Steampunk Dogs

Drawing

By Jeffrey Stains

Copyright©2016 Jeffrey Stains

All Rights Reserved

Table of contents

Disclaimer

While all attempts have been made to verify the information provided in this book, the author does assume any responsibility for errors, omissions, or contrary interpretations of the subject matter contained within. The information provided in this book is for educational and entertainment purposes only. The reader is responsible for his or her own actions and the author does not accept any responsibilities for any liabilities or damages, real or perceived, resulting from the use of this information.

The trademarks that are used are without any consent, and the publication of the trademark is without permission or backing by the trademark owner. All trademarks and brands within this book are for clarifying purposes only and are the owned by the owners themselves, not affiliated with this document.

Introduction

You might be familiar with the genre of Steampunk as an art form. This genre has extended much beyond the literary forms. Even if you have not tried your hands on Steampunk drawings, you can learn from **Steampunk Dogs: Drawing Steampunk Dogs** with much ease.

The book has been written in such a manner that the amateur as well as expert artists can learn Steampunk drawings from it.

The initial chapters deal with some information on Steampunk as an art form. You will also find a chapter which mentions dogs depicted in various paintings by a few contemporary artists. The latter part of the book deals with the tutorials of various sketches of Steampunk dogs.

Dogs have been an indispensable part of the human society. They have been the loyal friend of human beings even when we had not learnt how to talk. The bond between both the beings extends much beyond the words. Even today, there are many people, who cannot talk or are in some way physically challenged. But, they have specially trained dogs, who take care of their daily communication with others and their domestic chores as well.

Before drawing dogs in Steampunk forms, you must master your drawings in their basic anatomy. Only then, you will be able to draw them with perfection in this genre. Just like you try to attain perfection in human anatomy as a basic step of drawing and sketching, you must do the same with the drawing of dogs as well. In that case, you will be able to draw the animal in various positions and also give different gestures to them.

You might have seen a variety of photographs on Internet which shows dogs and other animals displaying emotions on their faces just like humans. The animals have been doing it always. It's just that we have more access to still cameras and video cameras to capture such precious moments. You can also capture such moments with your pet, if you have one and use them as an inspiration to your drawings. In the first section of this book, you will find a mention of one such dog, Snoopy, which is an icon of dogs to kids till date. The artist drew inspiration for this cartoon of dog from his own pet only.

A great artist must have an eye for great photographs as well. If you do not own a DSLR, you can use the camera of your smartphone. The lenses of Smartphone these days are well equipped to capture such moments. Utilize your resources to the best extent possible and you will find no dearth of inspiration to draw Steampunk sketches. Just look around and you will get the point. Read as much as you can about this unique genre and you will attain perfection as the times flies.

Steampunk, as an art form, requires a keen eye of the artist for making drawings. You do not have to be an engineer to draw the parts of machinery and incorporate them in your drawings. Just a careful observation of the machinery around you is enough.

Go through the tutorials of this book to begin with the drawings of Steampunk dogs.

Good luck for your journey!

Section 1 The Basics of Steampunk

Chapter 1 - Steampunk as an Art Form

Steampunk had once been just a literary genre. But, now it has become a culture and style unto itself. Earlier, Steampunk used to be a thought of alternate history, which later evolved into an art movement, fashion, or more like a way of life. After the creative authors wrote novels after novels in the backdrop of Victorian era, the fans were inspired to pump life into the technology and beauty of Steampunk through fashion and art. And now, there is no dearth of such people, who adore this genre so much so that they have adopted a complete wardrobe like those of Steampunk characters, and their way of life is like a dream come true.

You can easily spot Steampunk art in various shapes and sizes, like redesigned laptops, pocket watches, houses and vehicles. Since one's art reveals one's identity, the scale of implementation of Steampunk in one's daily life depends on their imagination and passion. You may realize this art form in the sporty tinkering of a gadget or in the painting and designing of complex and vast Victorian utopias. Even if you are not an artist, just being an appreciator or a collector, you can adopt Steampunk art pieces in any shape and size.

Difference between Steampunk and Victorian art objects

If you want to find out the difference between Steampunk and Victorian art objects, you can do so by determining the inventiveness and technology of the art piece. Though there is a very heavy influence of Victorian styles on Steampunk objects, but the latter are modernized and re-imaged works. These two features set them apart. The dreamers of Victorian Era would often visualize that the Steampunk art forms should look like those of Victorian age. However, there are some obvious differences in both.

For beginners

If you are a beginner at Steampunk art objects, you must first of all determine the materials you should work with. The typical authentic materials used in the Victorian era were copper, brass, glass, leather, wood, etc. You can of course use other mediums because Steampunk is just a re-invention of Victorian era. However, if you stick to those typical materials, your objects would definitely get a more authentic Steampunk look.

You must avoid using plastic in real Steampunk objects, since it was invented much later. Standard accessories and additions may include objects like gears, rivets, chains, cogs and other industrial objects. However, you must include these objects only if they fit into your imagination, not just because you want to make your art forms "look" like Steampunk.

Your idea of Steampunk may not confirm to the notions of any other artist. But, the realization of your ideas of a futuristic Victorian society lies solely in your hands since the ideas of one artist are completely different for the other. If you want to endeavor your own art form, it is crucial that you do not get discouraged by the criticism of others and take them in good spirit. Sometimes, you may feel that the object you made or drew is not "Steampunk enough". At such times, you can improve your art rather than getting discouraged. You must stick to your inspiration and creativity if you really want to modify your art as a manifestation of what the genre of Steampunk signifies for you.

Chapter 2 - Dogs in Art

Dogs have been portrayed in various art forms since ages. They have been a true and loyal friend of the mankind. And, even the humans have not hesitated to accessorize their four legged friends to the best extent possible. Some of them are friendly enough to let you do whatever you want to do. Some of them even pose for the photographs and paintings. But, not all dogs are so well behaved. But whatsoever, dogs will still remain the love objects of humans.

Here, we have mentioned some of the dogs portrayed in various paintings. You might recognize some of these art works. Their inspiration sets off beyond the love of the artist.

1. **Pride of Parenthood by Norman Rockwell**

    Norman Rockwell many a times included dogs in some of the iconic scenes of the family life of America. His own dog was a mutt called Pitter, who accompanied him while he worked on his paintings. Rockwell always said that an artist should paint dogs as carefully as they paint people.

2. Snoopy by Charles Schulz

Spike was the childhood dog of Charles Schulz, who later became the inspiration for the iconic Snoopy. Spike was in a strange habit of eating abnormal things. When the artist was 15 year old, he sent a hand drawn picture of Spike to *Ripley's Believe It or Not!* It explained how Spike had swallowed tacks, razor blades and pins in whole form. But, he was still in perfect health. Unlike the beagle, Snoopy, the pet of Charles was a pointer. But, his black ears and white coat are suggestive of the adorable character.

3. Dancing Dogs by Keith Haring

During the 1980s, Keith Haring rose to fame when he posted his art work in public. Some of them were also revealed in the subways of New York. You can frequently witness dancing dogs in his work, which are more like a trademark of his brand name. The dogs of Haring appear like humans since they can be seen dancing on two legs. However, it is interesting to see them even larger than human beings when the two are portrayed together.

4. Lump by Picasso

Picasso had a Dachshund called Lump. David Duncan, his photographer friend called the relationship between the two was called a love affair. Lump originally belonged to Duncan but after he visited Picasso's house in 1957, he dwelled there for 6 years. Interestingly, out of so many dogs owned by him, Picasso fed and held only Lump. And the dog died just ten days prior to Picasso.

5. Their Master's Voice by Michael Sowa

Michael Sowa, a contemporary artist as well as illustrator features many animals frequently in his works. In the paintings of this German artist, the animals are portrayed as main subject and they are seen competing or replacing humans. The animals, especially dogs are found carrying out human business like surfing or skating such as in his painting, Laptop Sheep.

Section 2 Steampunk Dogs
Chapter 1 – Bram

Before drawing Steampunk dogs, you must practice drawing dog figures in general. It is important to understand their anatomy. Once you get the hang of anatomy of dogs, it becomes easier to insert parts of machinery in the drawings of dogs to make them more like Steampunk. Let us start with a few Steampunk drawings of dogs. After going through a few chapters, you can make your own drawings and modify them with the machinery of your choice.

Step 1

This dog, Bram, is drawn from the left profile of its body. You can see the last step of this tutorial for reference to sketch the whole body roughly. Draw a light outline of the body of the dog. Highlight the muzzle, nose and floppy ears of Bram.

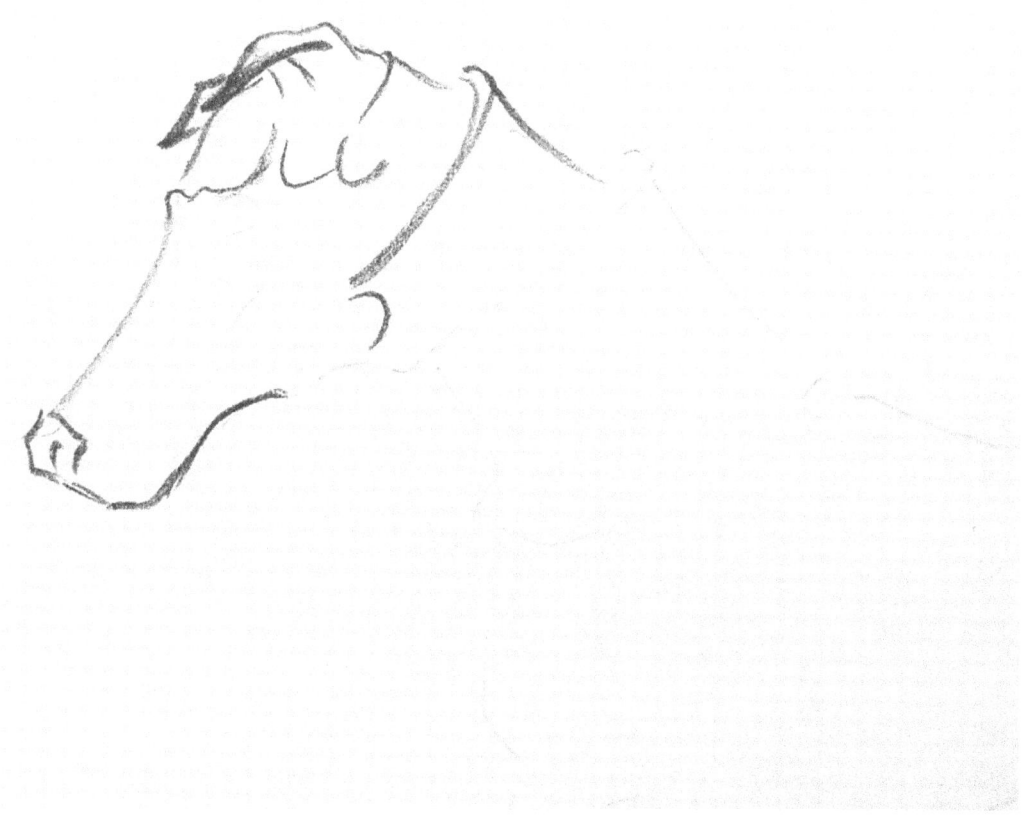

Step 2

Draw a belt on the nape of its head. Draw the eye visible from your perspective. Draw a few fasteners on the cheeks of Bram.

After drawing all these objects on the head, give shading on the head, cheeks and nose. In all the drawings of dogs, we will keep the shading to minimum to highlight the Steampunk character of the animals.

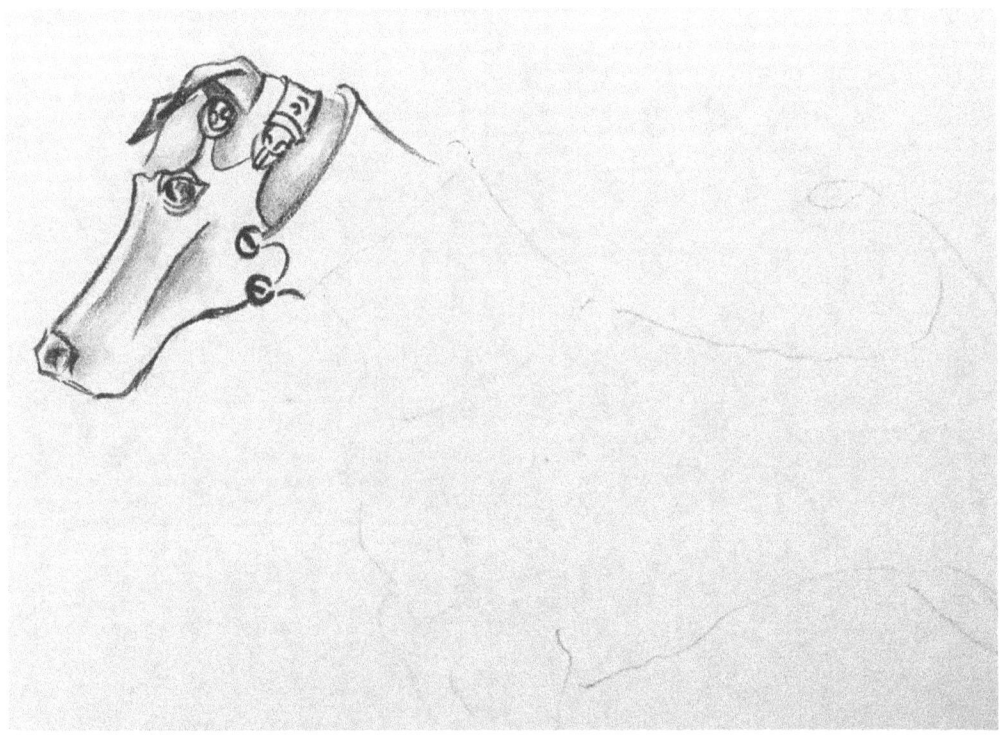

Step 3

Draw the metal plates on the neck of Bram, covering his neck throughout. Highlight the upper rim of the plates. Shade these plates with darker shading near the nape and lighter shading in the remaining portion. The shading is vertical in direction. This is important with the perspective of showing the quality of the metal and its shine.

Notice that the plate is bent according to the body of the animal.

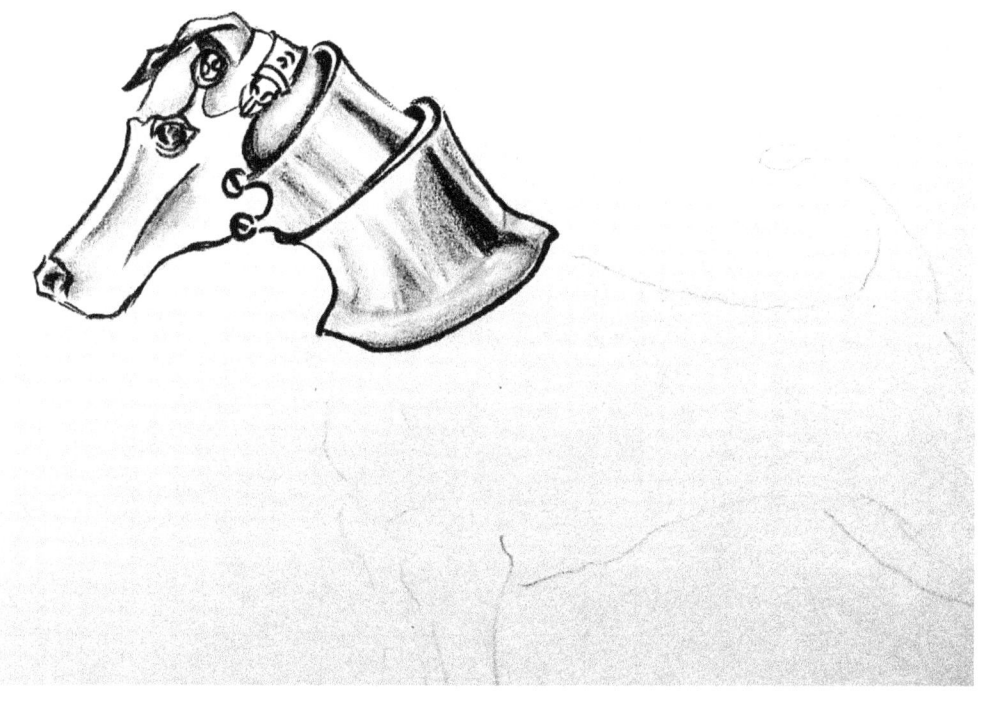

Step 4

Darken the outline of the remaining body of Bram. In the area of tail of Bram, draw a fastener at the tip of the tail and another fastener at the thicker portion where the tail is emerging from the body.

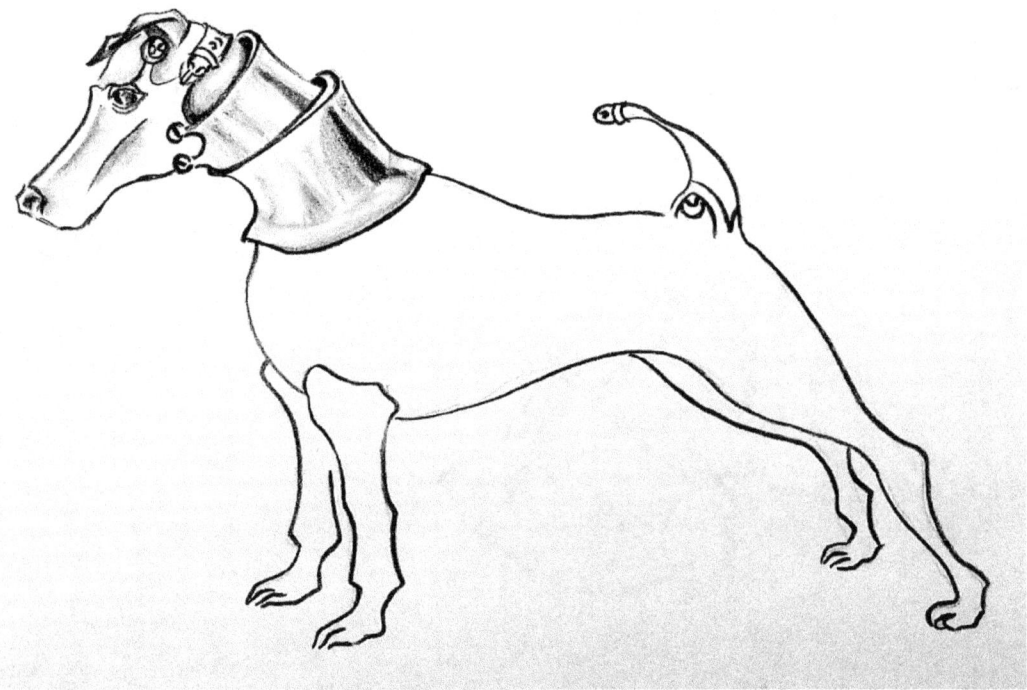

Step 5

Divide the body of the dog into two parts by drawing a link as if a metal casing is entwined over the other. Draw some running stitches along the edges of this division. Draw two fasteners along the edges of the semicircle drawn on the division. Draw one bigger fastener in the hollow of the semicircle.

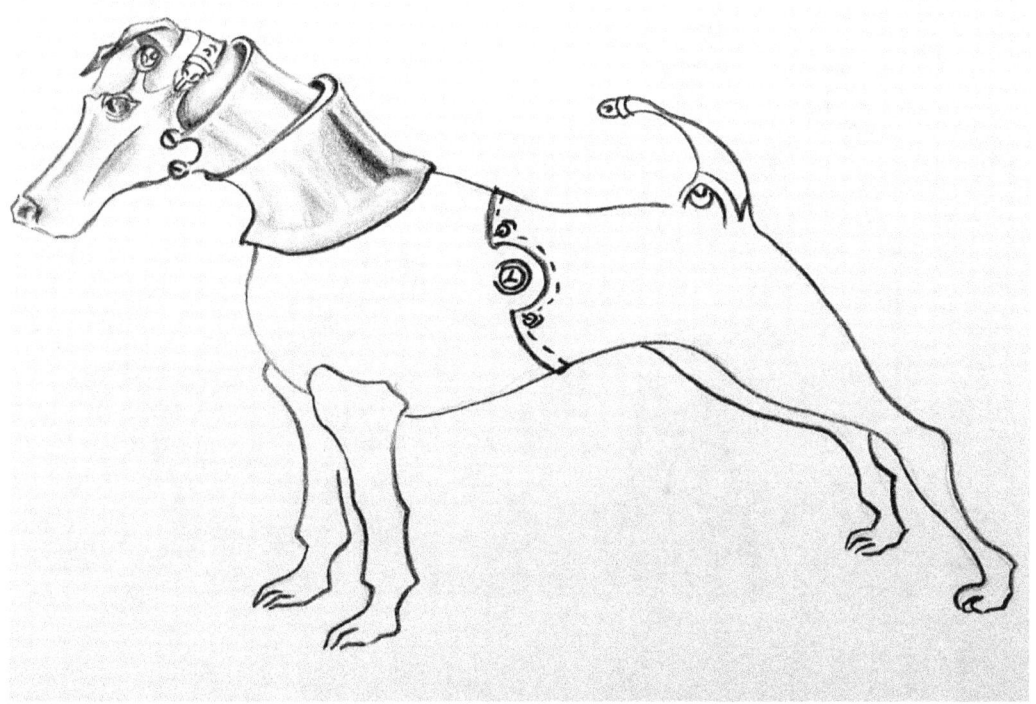

Step 6

As we did in the previous step, draw a metal casing on the front leg of Bram and also draw some smaller casings on the same leg beneath the larger casing. Give shading in the front division of the body. Draw a third portion in the croup of the dog in almost "V" shape.

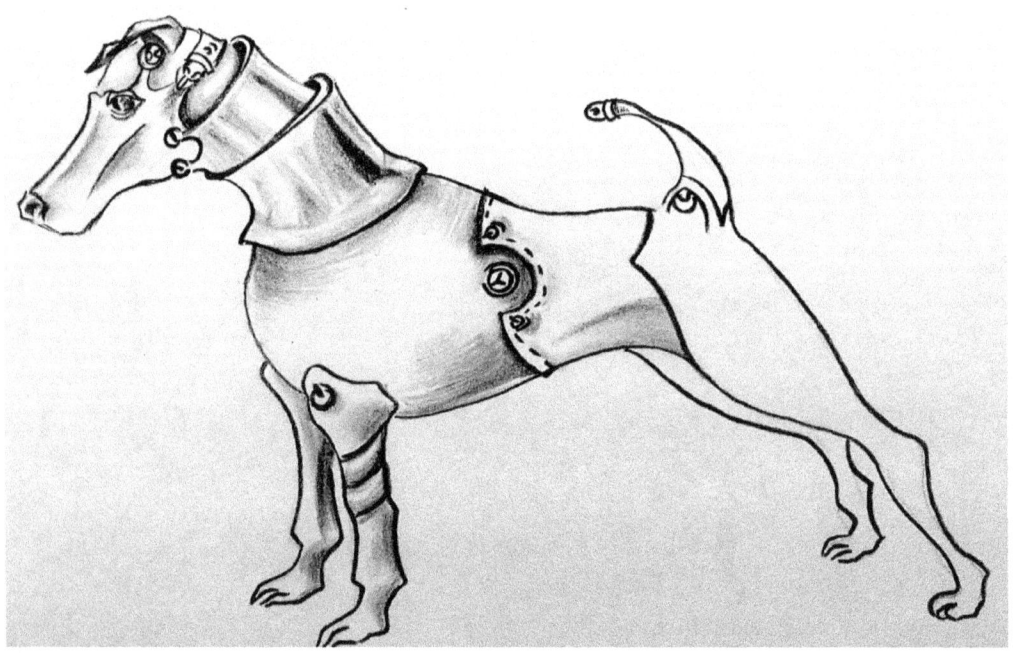

Step 7

In the third division, draw three fasteners like you would do at the tips of a triangle and connect them with the lines as shown in the picture. Draw a few running stitches in this portion.

At the origin of the tail, draw a hollow rough triangle and darken it leaving a small circular portion. In this circular portion, draw a darkened circle. Look at the picture for reference.

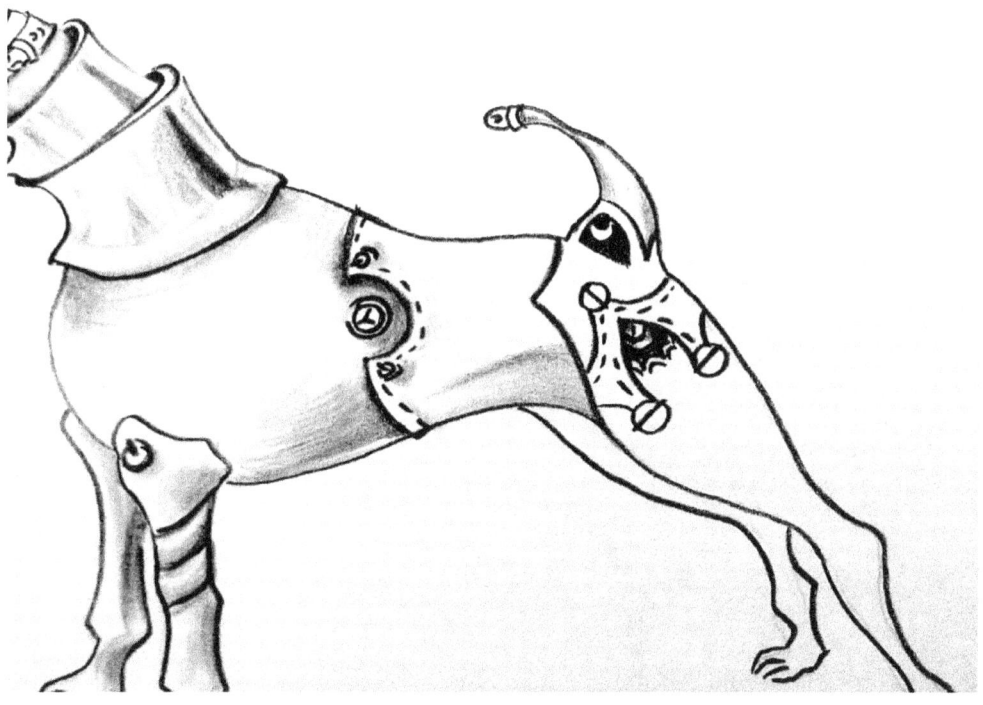

Step 8

Give shading in one of the hind legs of Bram.

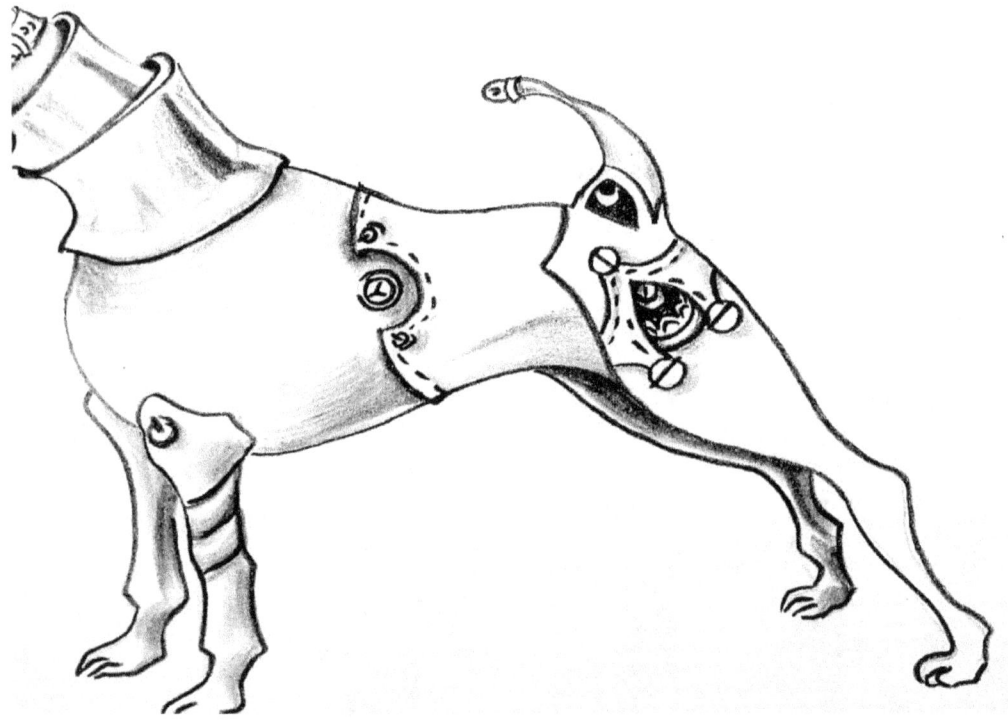

Step 9

In the hind leg facing you, draw a fastener at the joint of the leg. Divide the casings drawn on this leg as shown in the picture. Give shading in the remaining portion of the leg.

The Steampunk dog, Bram, is complete.

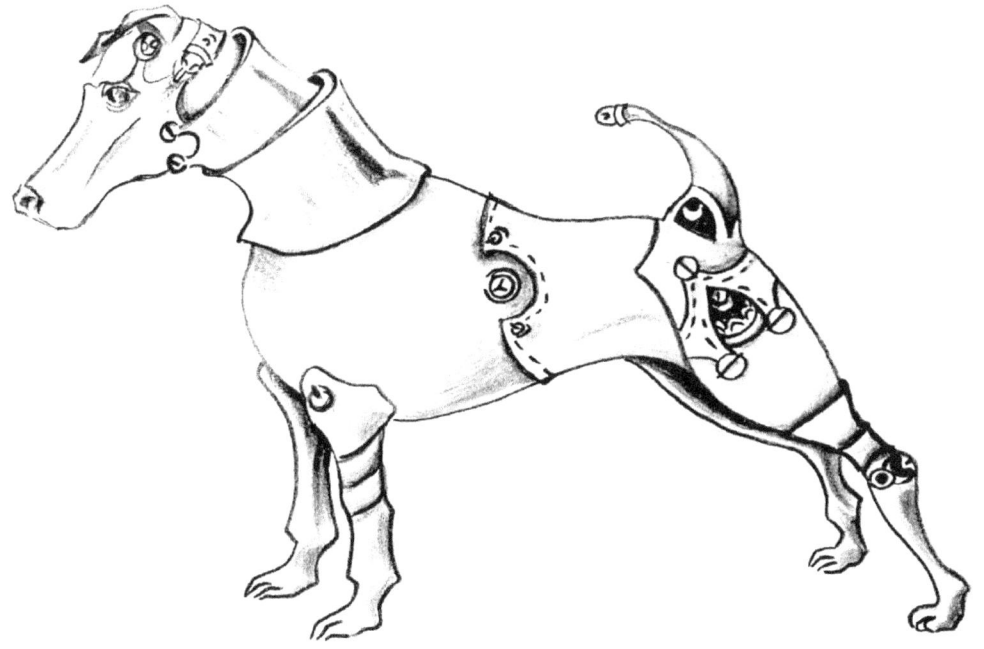

Chapter 2 – Hugo

Hugo is one of those Steampunk dogs, who are active beyond expectations. It has sharp features and a stiff body. Even the floppy ears are always erect to stay attentive to the sounds of its environment.

Step 1

Draw a cross sign to mark the position of the eyes of this dog called, Hugo. We will draw him from the left profile of his face. Draw the outline of his face, ears, muzzle and nose.

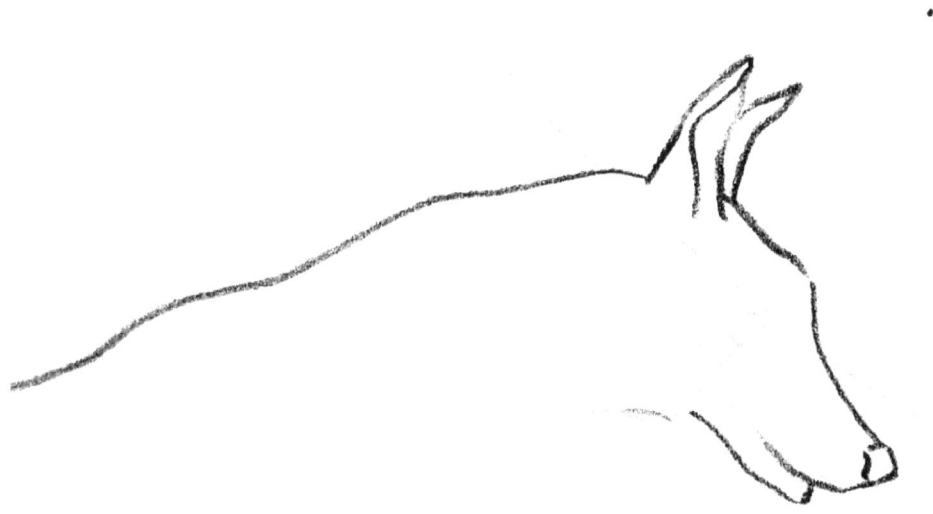

Step 2

Erase the cross sign after drawing the eyes. Give shading in the muzzle and near the lips.

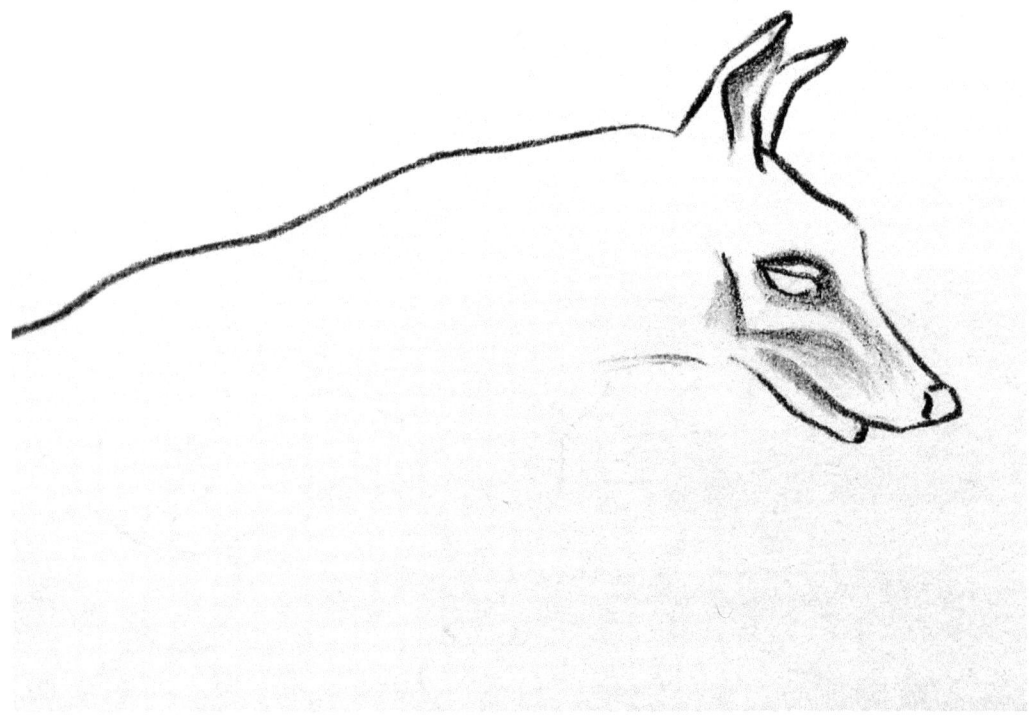

Step 3

Carve out a portion in the neck of Hugo as shown in the picture. Draw two fasteners on the head, one large and one small.

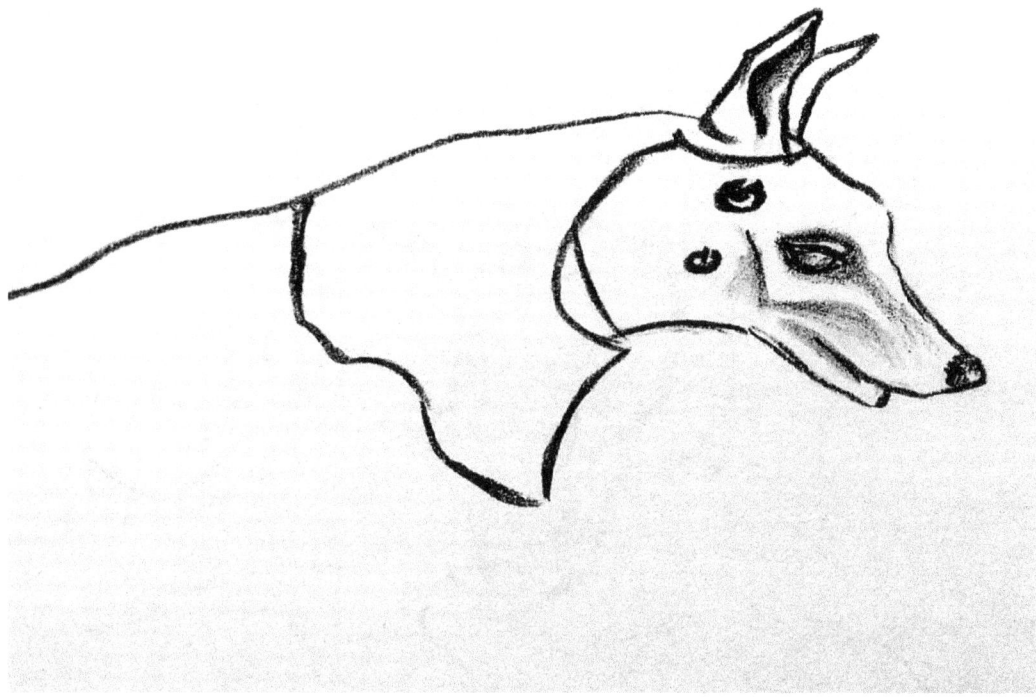

Step 4

Along the division you made in the previous step, draw a strap as shown in illustration. Draw a large fastener near the nape of the neck. Draw a horizontal "V" shape along this fastener.

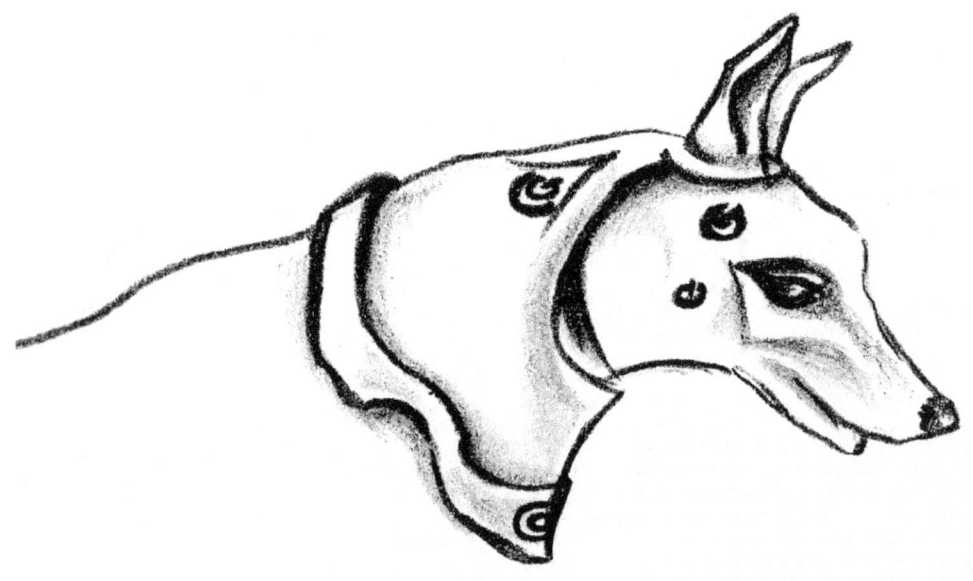

Step 5

Give shading in the division and the front portion of the dog's body. Draw the outline of the remaining body of the dog.

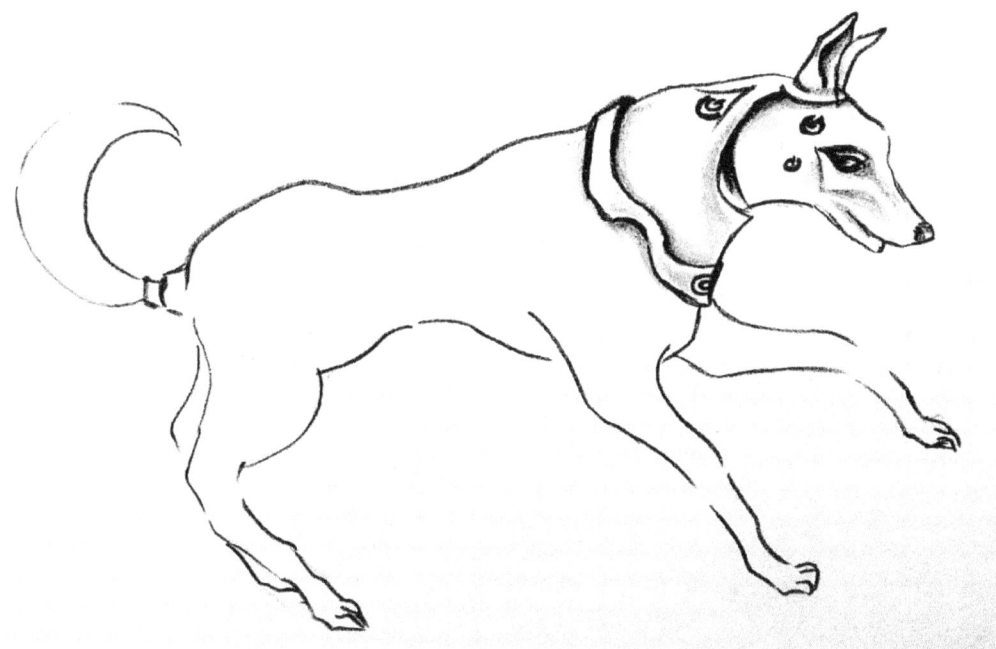

Step 6

Draw several divisions in the body of Hugo as shown in the illustration using metal casings overlapped over each other. Lay special emphasis on the tail.

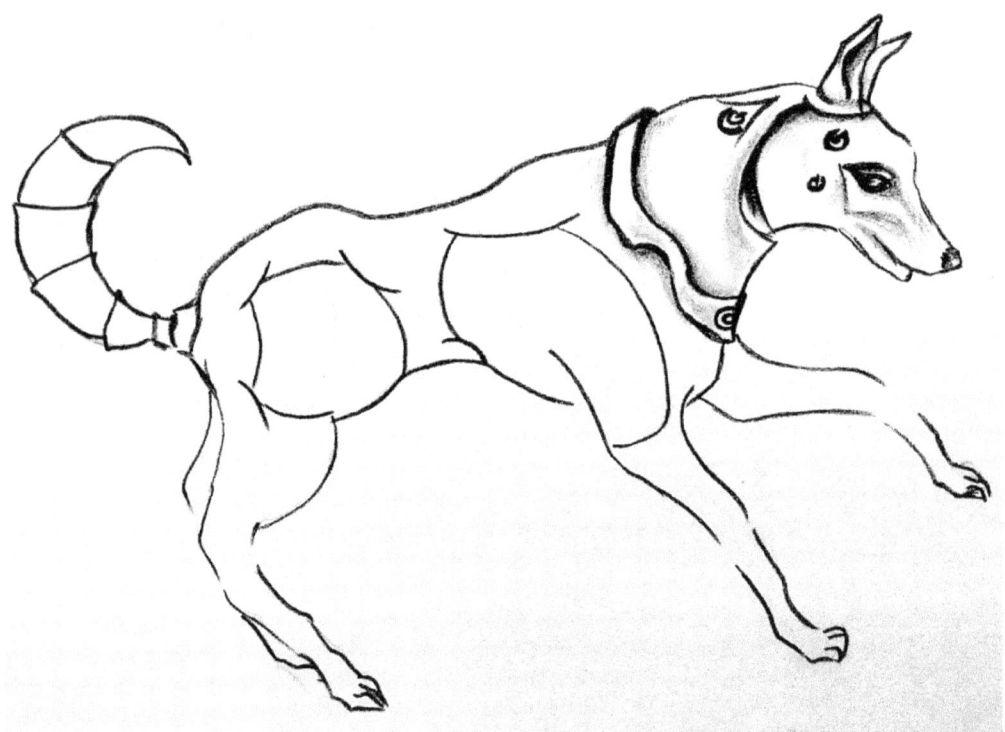

Step 7

In the two hollow portions shown in the picture, draw some bearings close to each other. Give some suggestions of such bearings in the legs as well.

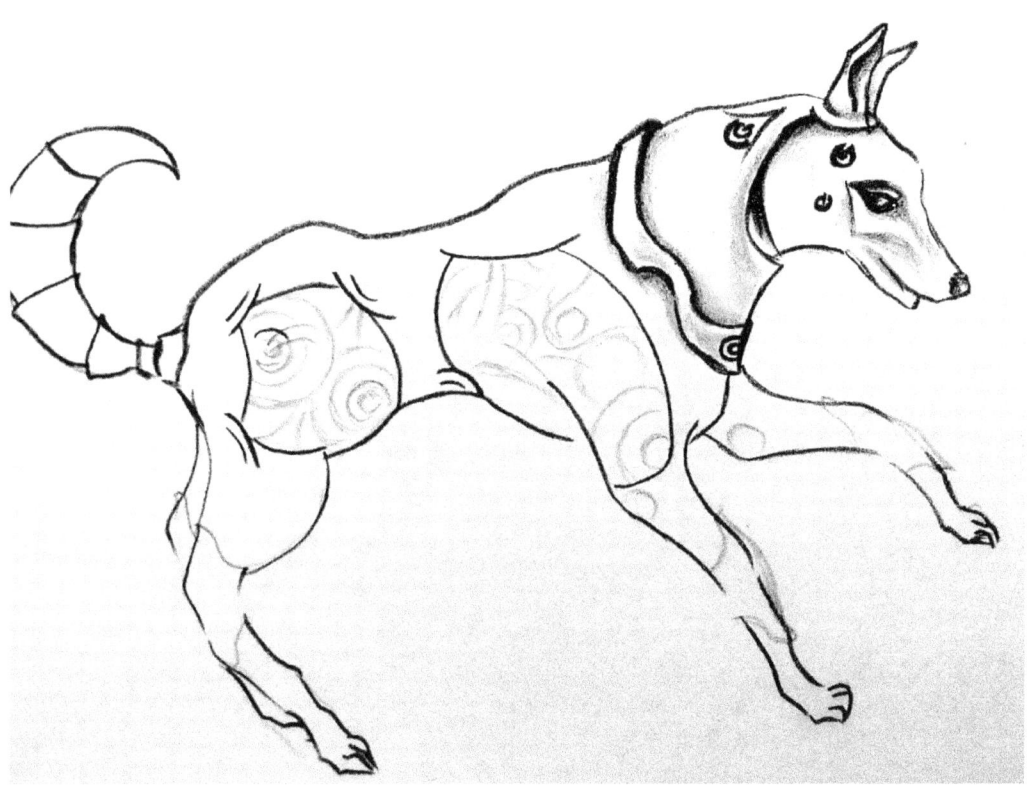

Step 8

Darken the hollow portions of the bearings and highlight the outlines of the same.

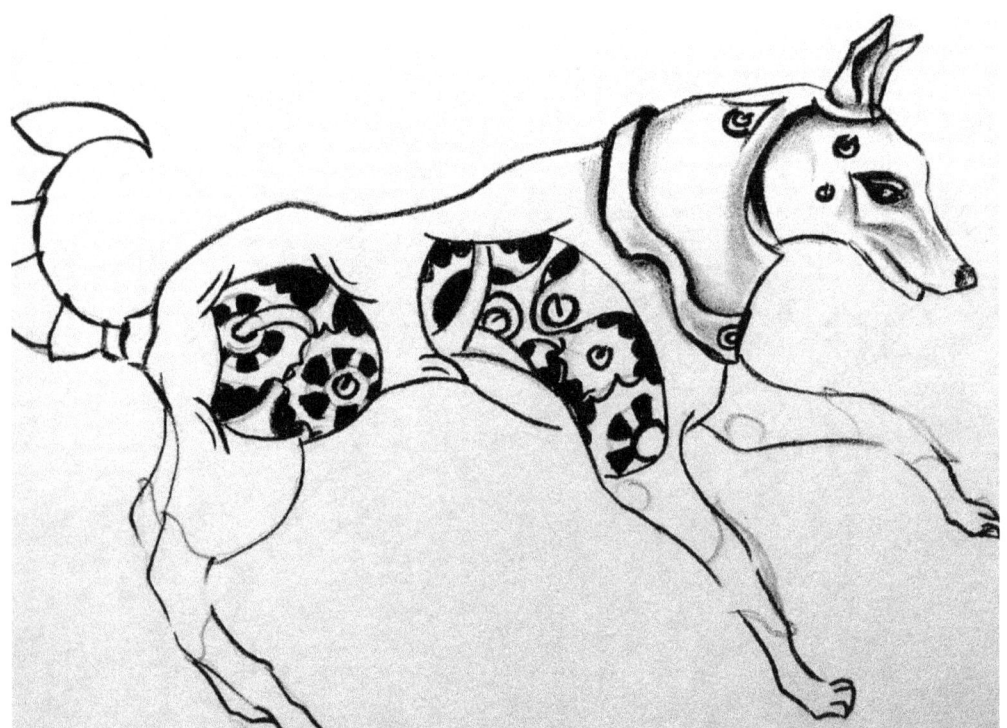

Step 9

Draw metal plates on the joints of all the legs of Hugo. The plates are designed to protect the legs of this fighter dog.

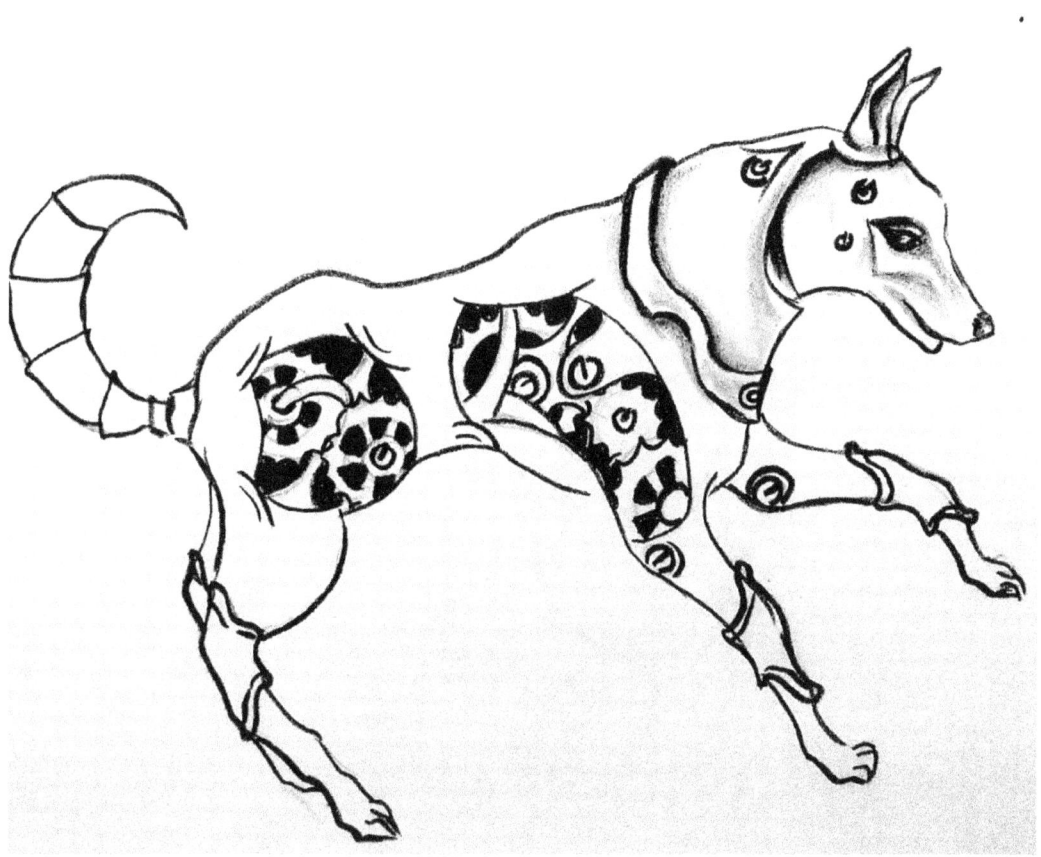

Step 10

Give shading in the metal plates of the tail. Take care to give darker shading around the lines and lighter shading in the remaining portion of the plates.

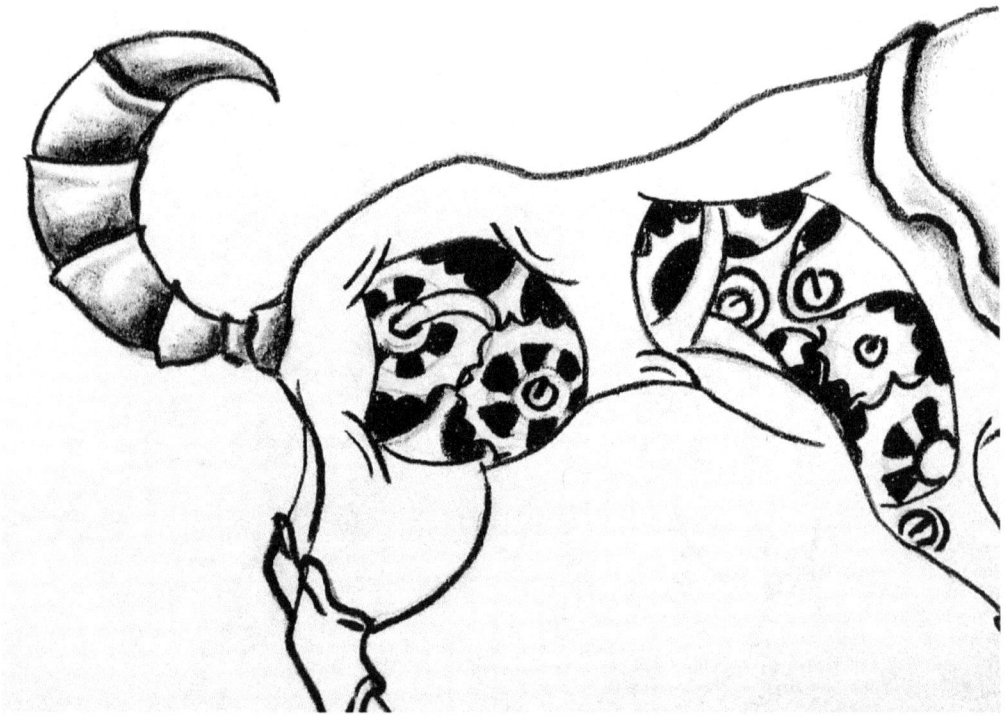

Step 11

Give shading in the required areas of the remaining drawing to complete the sketch of Steampunk fighter dog, Hugo.

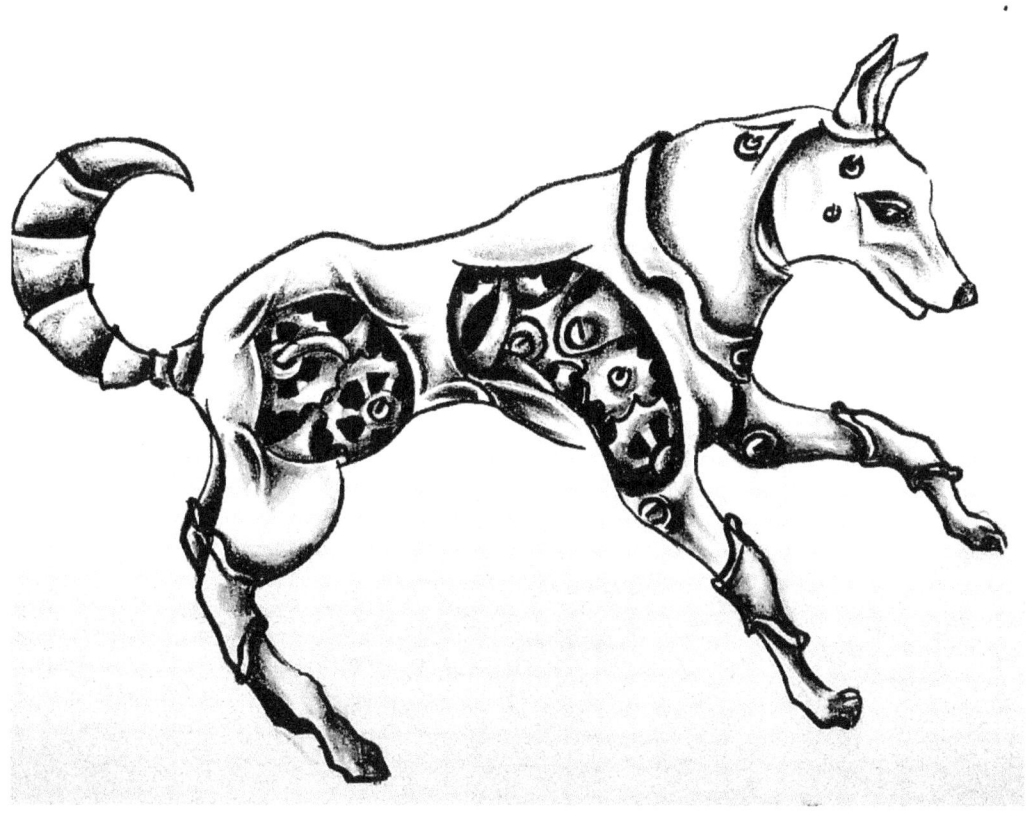

Chapter 3 - Jules

This one is a cute Steampunk dog called, Jules. He will not fight with anyone. You can rather carry him in your lap and enjoy cuddling him.

Step 1

Draw a light outline of the body of this animal. The muzzle is a little larger than normal. The eyes are also bigger and the floppy ears are hanging in a relaxed position.

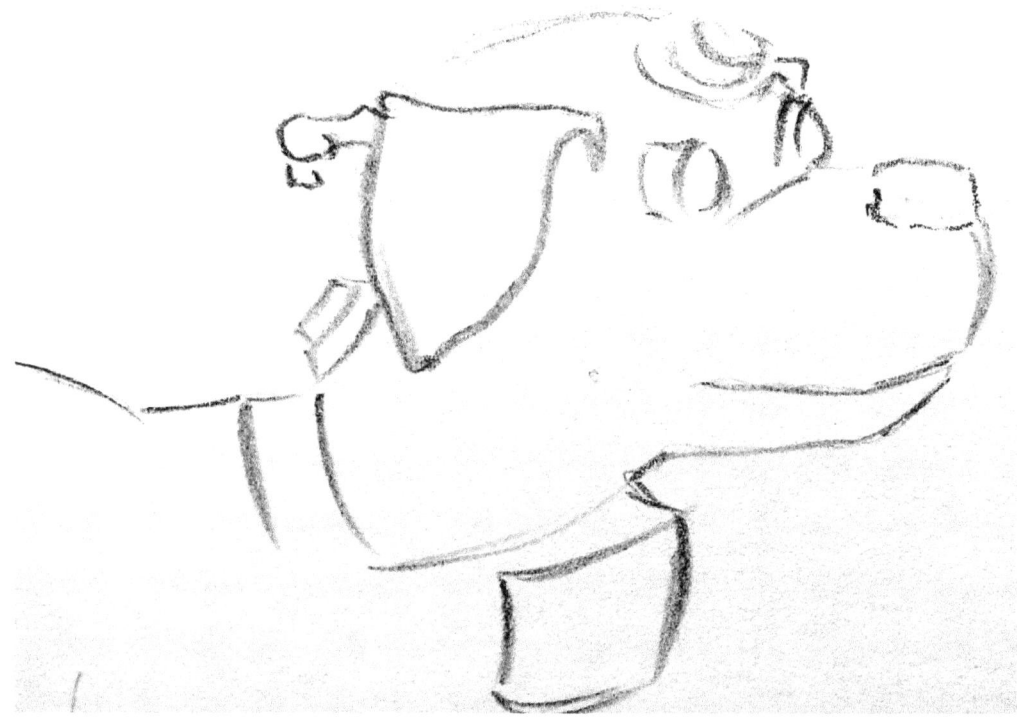

Step 2

Darken the outlines of the face, ears and nose. Draw two large gears in perspective in place of the eyes. Draw a larger gear in the forehead with some metal chips around it. Draw a strip near the nose and some bold lines on this strip.

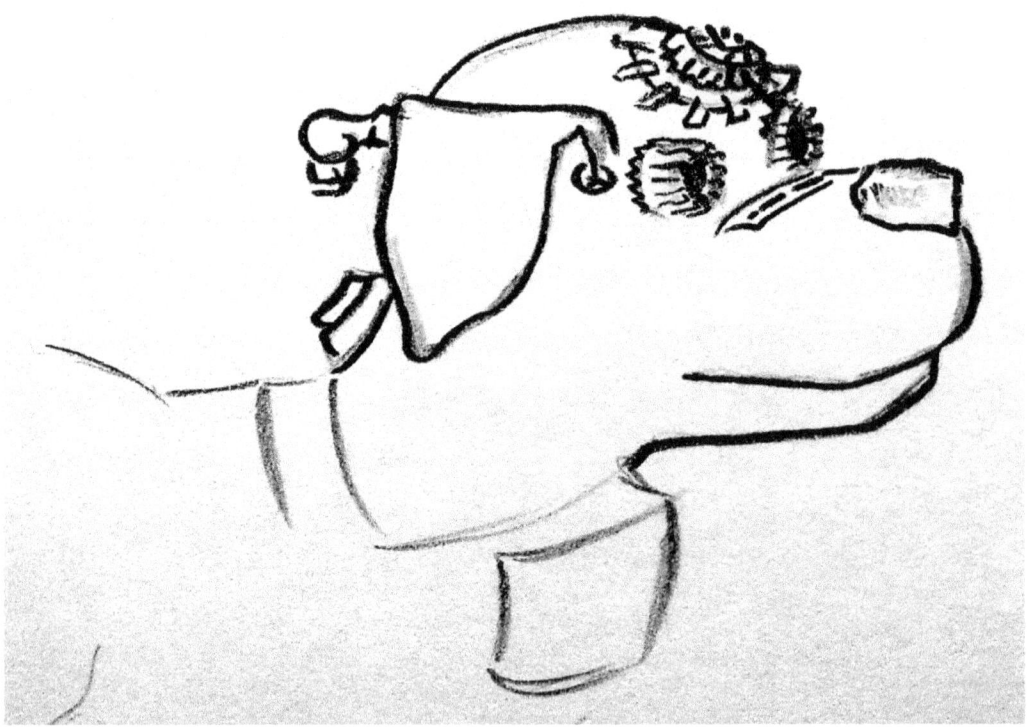

Step 3

Darken the outline of the remaining body of Jules. Draw a strap of fasteners around the neck. A metal plate is also there along the shoulder of the dog. Draw a coiled wire from the back side of the head to the nape of the neck. Notice the antenna on the tip of the tail.

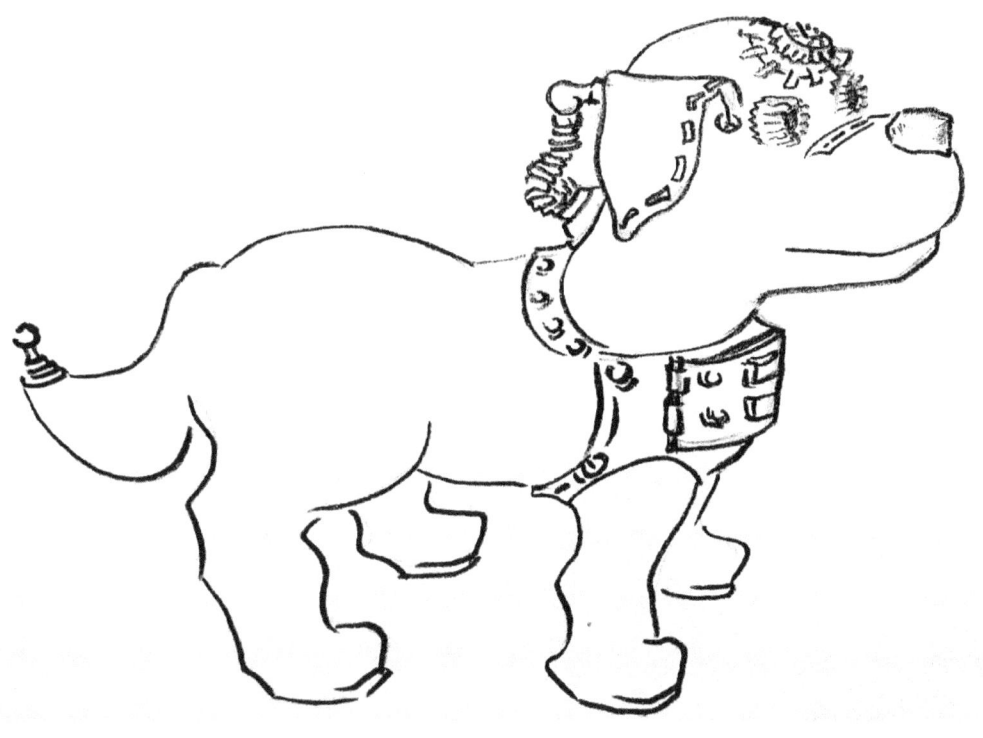

Step 4

Give shading in the front body of Jules and the hind leg facing you. Draw two large fasteners on the front leg facing you.

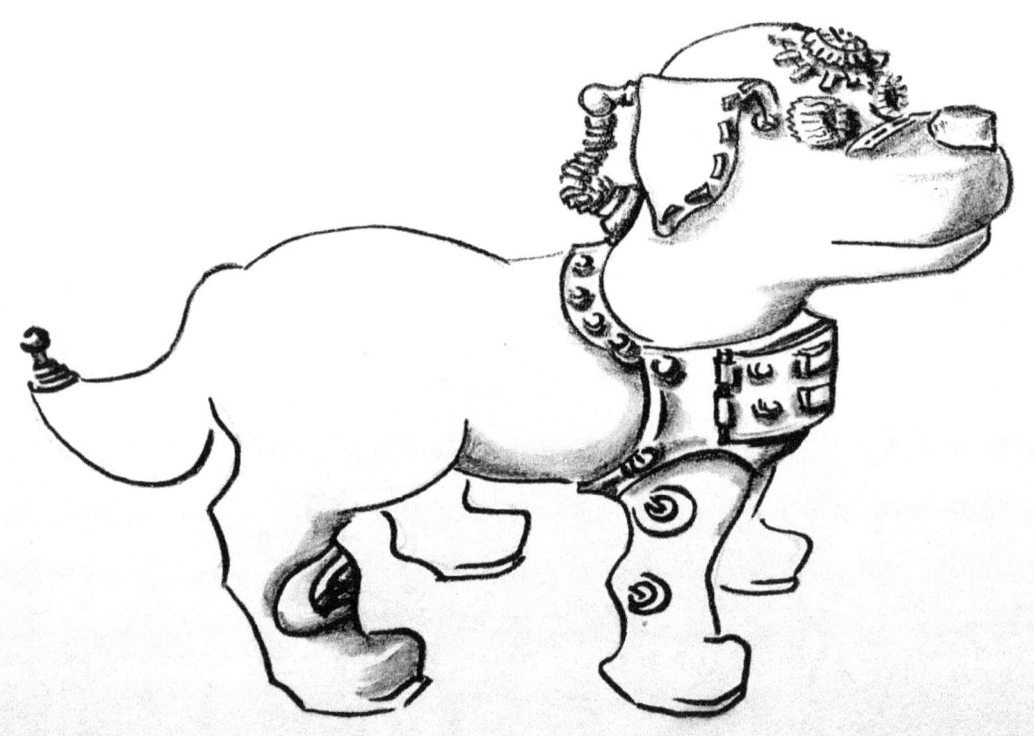

Step 5

Give shading in the rest of the legs of Jules. Draw a few running chips on the floppy ear of the dog. Give shading around them too. On the chest portion, draw a bearing with its teeth protruding outwards. Notice the small casings emerging from the center of this bearing.

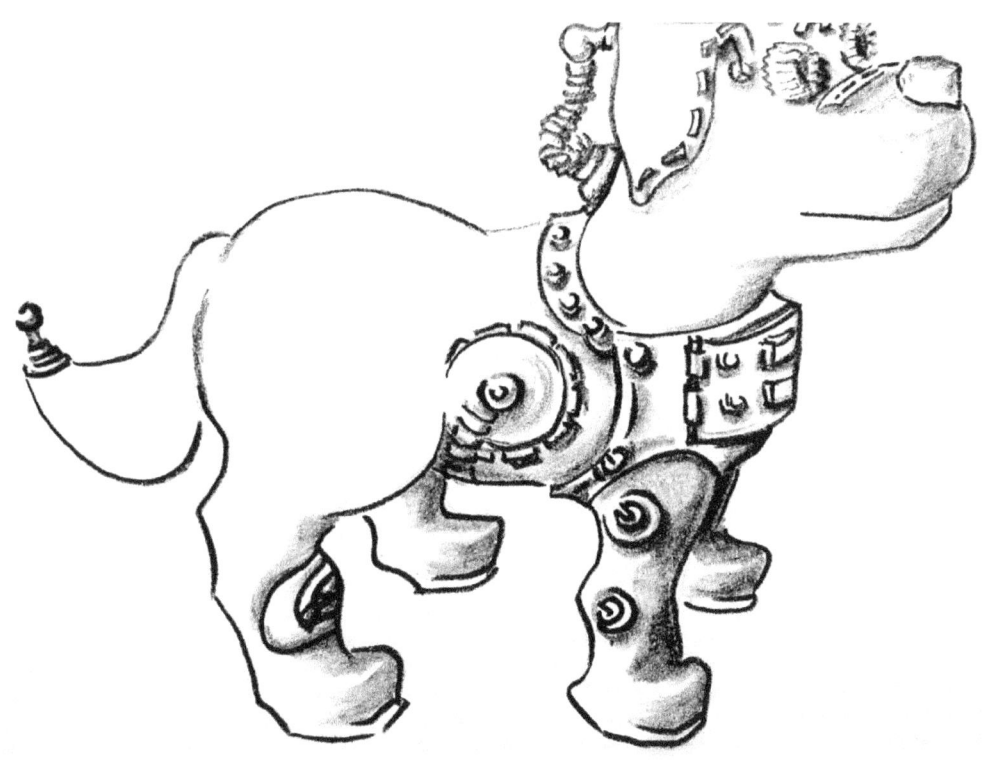

Step 6

Give shading in the remaining body of Jules. The sketch of cute Steampunk

dog, Jules is complete.

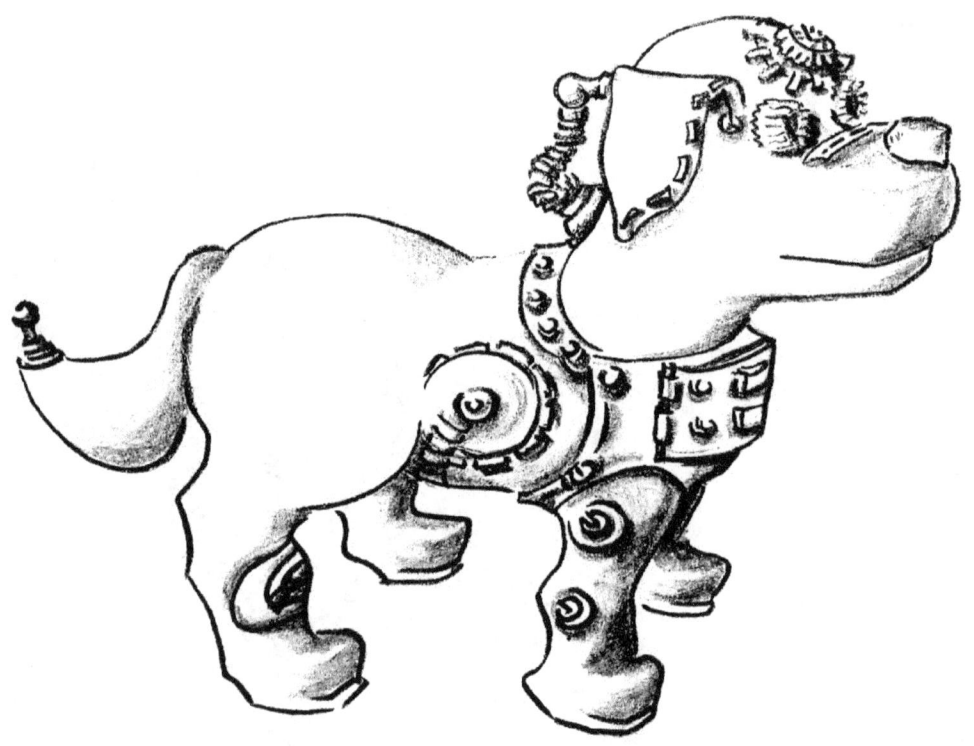

Chapter 4 – Phineas

This Steampunk dog named, Phineas, is modestly attentive to the commands of its master. Sometimes, it takes over a mission all by himself. But, at other times, it becomes very lazy, so much so, that it just wants to rest and sleep.

Step 1

Draw a light outline of the body of Phineas. Give some suggestions of the accessories of this dog. There is an antenna fixed near the left eye of Phineas. The floppy ear of the animal is shown in a resting position.

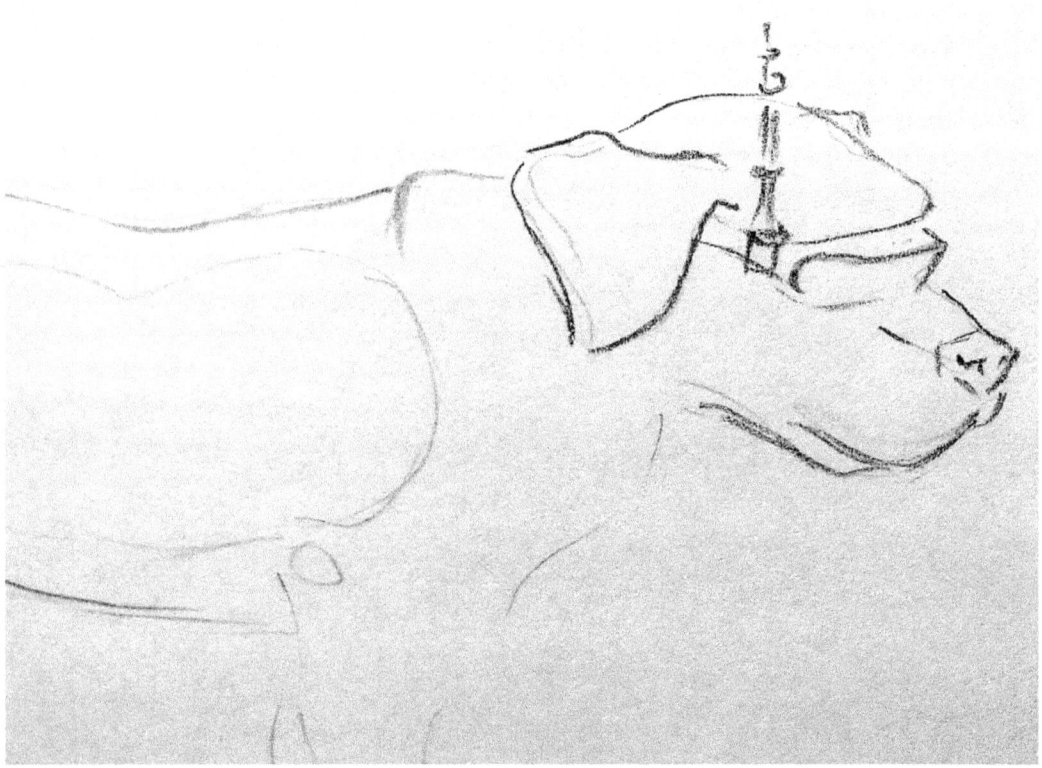

Step 2

Draw a triangular strip, with fasteners on its edges, on the forehead of Phineas. Draw a similar strip above the nose as well. Give shading in the goggles placed on the eyes. Give shading in the antenna as well. The breaks at various points in the antenna should be shaded carefully.

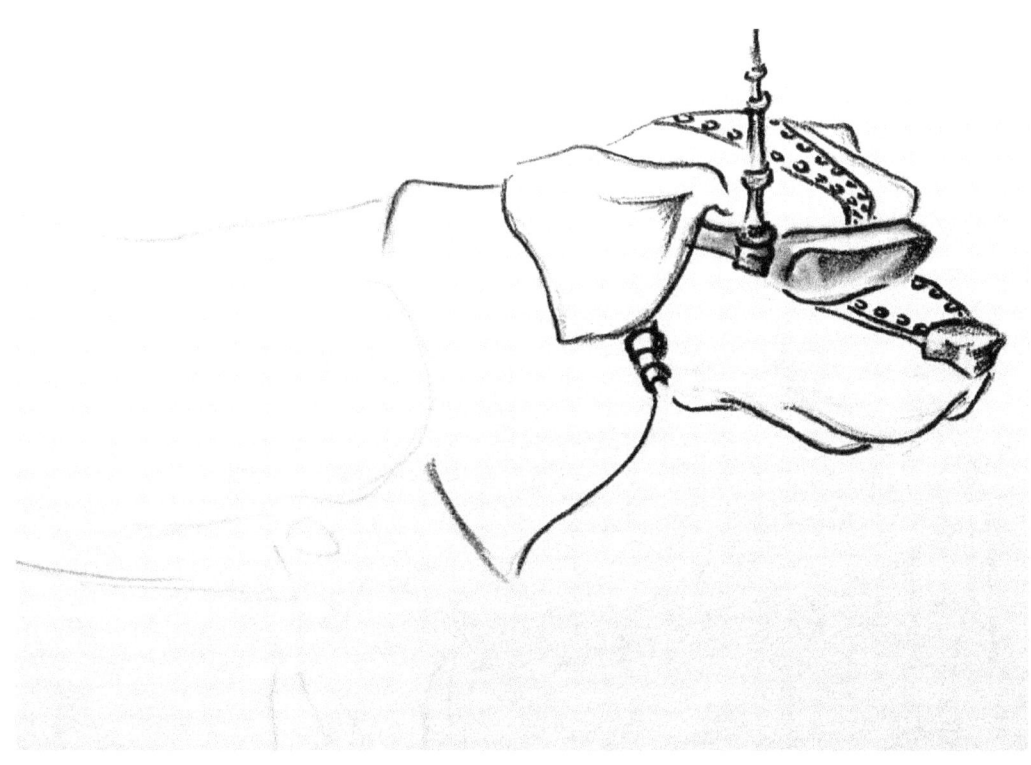

Step 3

Highlight the final outline of the body of the dog.

Carve out a hollow in the center of the body of Phineas. In this hollow portion, draw some gears connected with each other with the help of shafts. Draw a belt like strap on the shoulder. Depict a gear on the loin. Draw some fasteners on the hind leg facing you. Draw on fastener in such a manner that it is shown connected to a fastener above it and the strip below it.

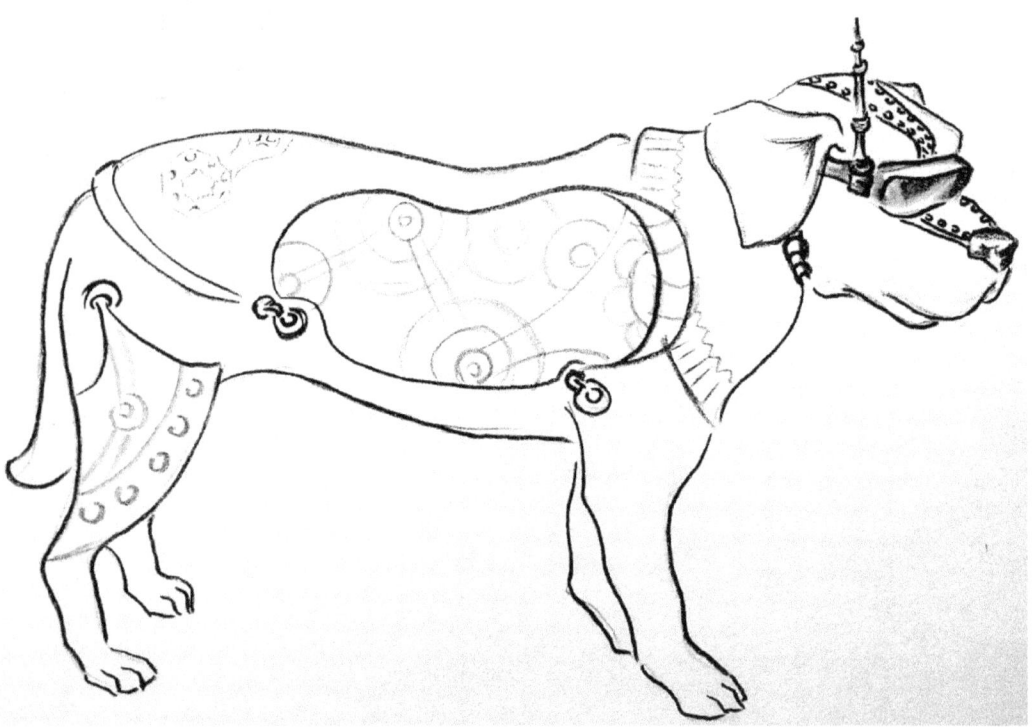

Step 4

Darken the hollow portions of the gears in the center of the body. In the center of the gears in this area, draw small circles, depicting fasteners connecting the shafts with each other. The shaft near the shoulder of the dog is broader than the others and contains a separate bearing on it. Highlight the bearing on the loin and connect it to a bearing partly shown here.

Highlight the strap of fasteners on the hind leg facing you. Also, emphasize the fasteners near this strap.

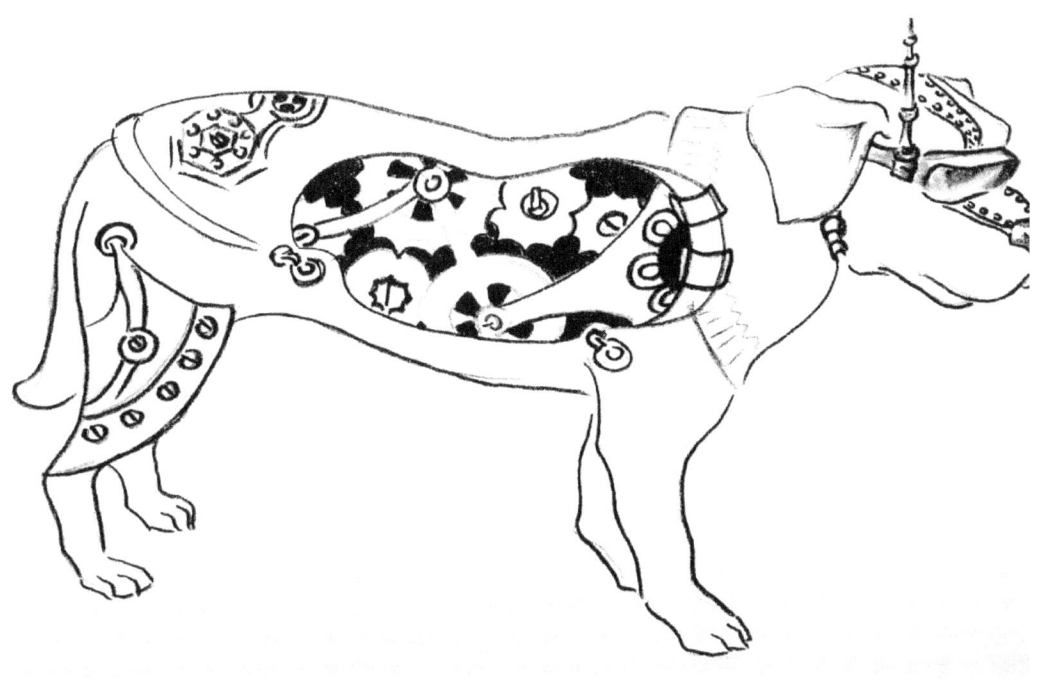

Step 5

Give shading in the body of the animal as depicted in the illustration. The Steampunk dog, Phineas, is complete.

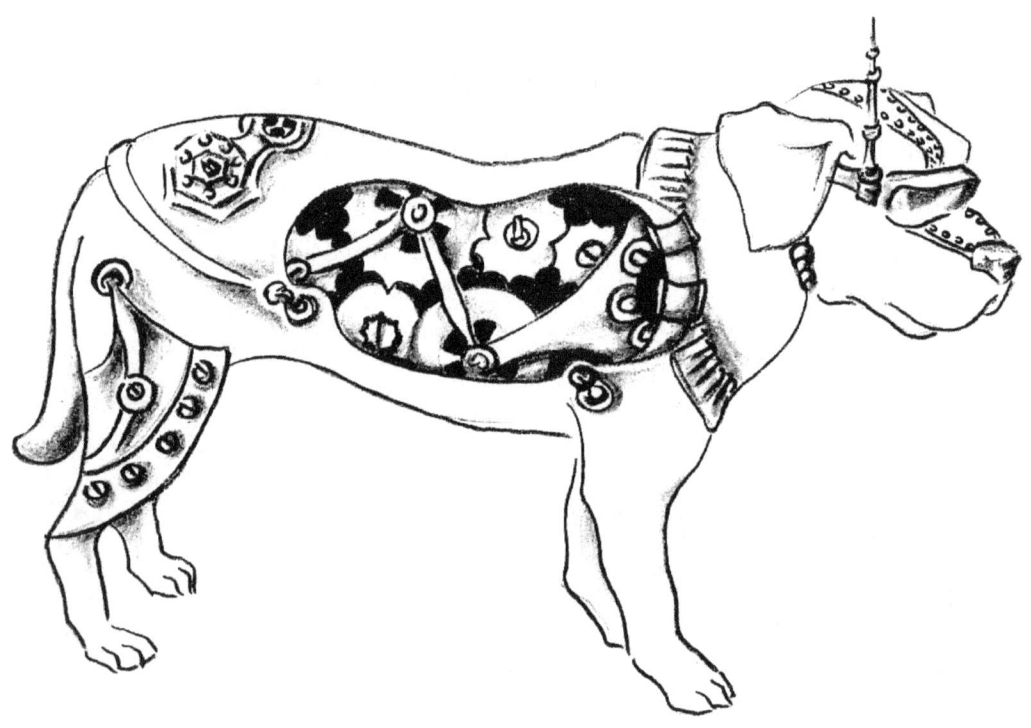

Chapter 5 - Granger

This Steampunk dog is known as Granger. It is quite dangerous to poke him too much as he would not hesitate to attack you. You need to draw the sharp features of this warrior dog with precision to make the best of it.

Step 1

Draw a rough draft of the body of Granger. The ears of this dog are smaller in comparison to others but are very attentive, not hanging down in rest.

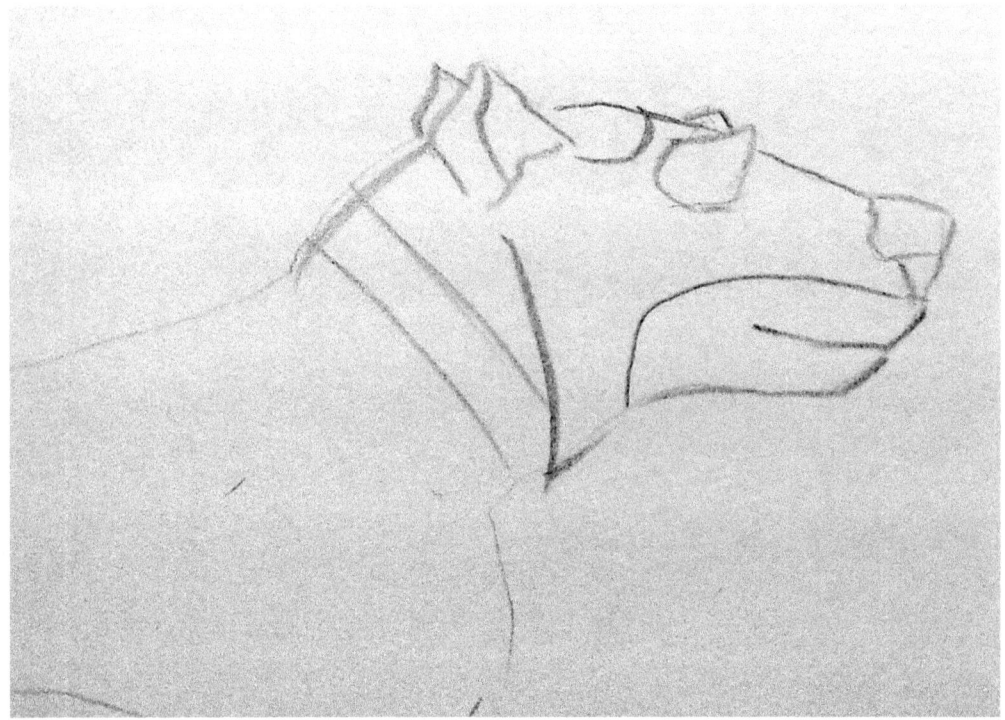

Step 2

Darken the outline of the body of Granger. The tail of this animal consists of large scales overlapping each other as shown in the picture. His tail is much more powerful than the other dogs. The eyes are covered with lenses, with the help of which, Granger can see much beyond his normal eye sight.

His ears are rather smaller but have significant strength and are erect at all times. The nose is drawn a little bigger than normal.

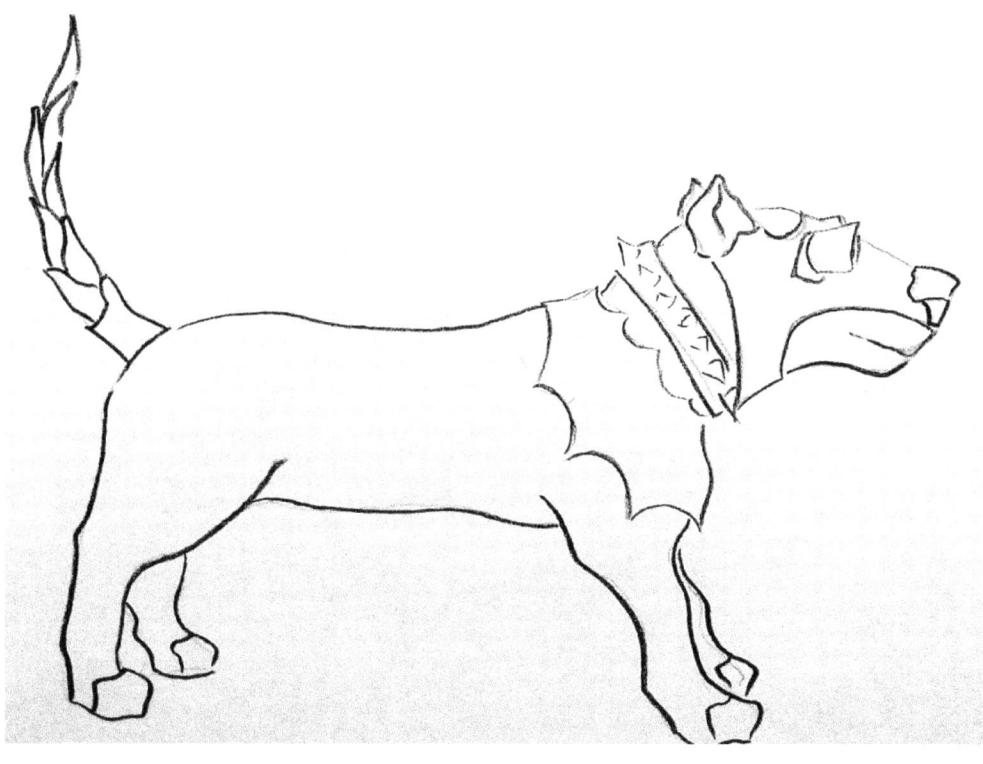

Step 3

Draw a metal casing on the head of Granger. Draw some fasteners along the edges of this casing. Draw some small chips on the nose of this dog. On the lenses drawn on the eye, draw similar chips as drawn on the nose.

Draw a belt with protruding spikes on the neck of the dog. Draw another metal plate on the shoulder and depict some fasteners on it as shown in the picture.

On the chest, draw a broad belt with a buckle and piercings.

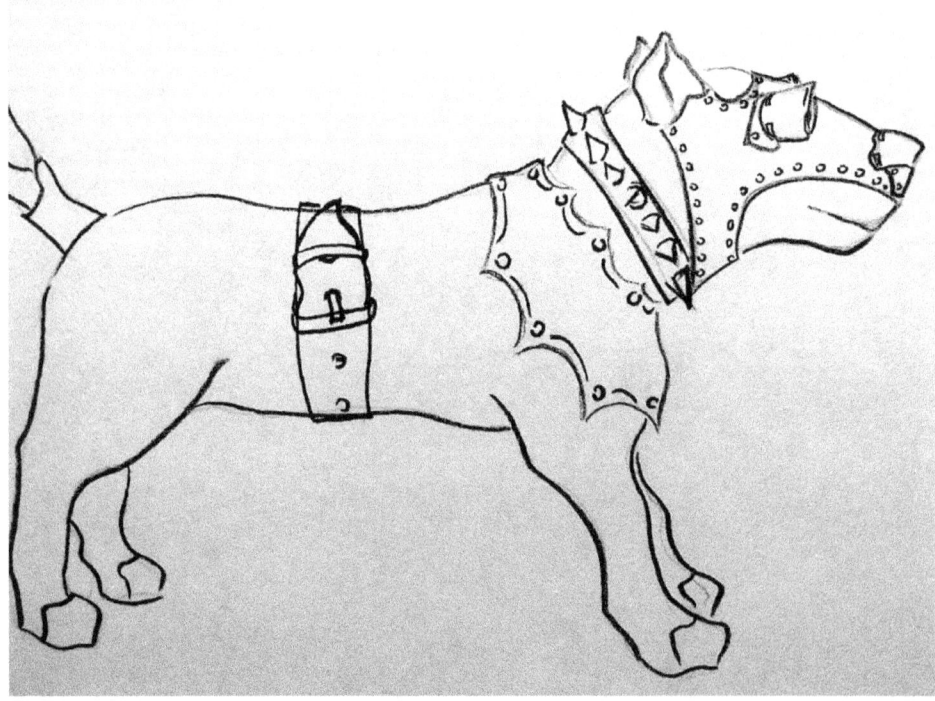

Step 4

Draw fasteners on each scale of the tail.

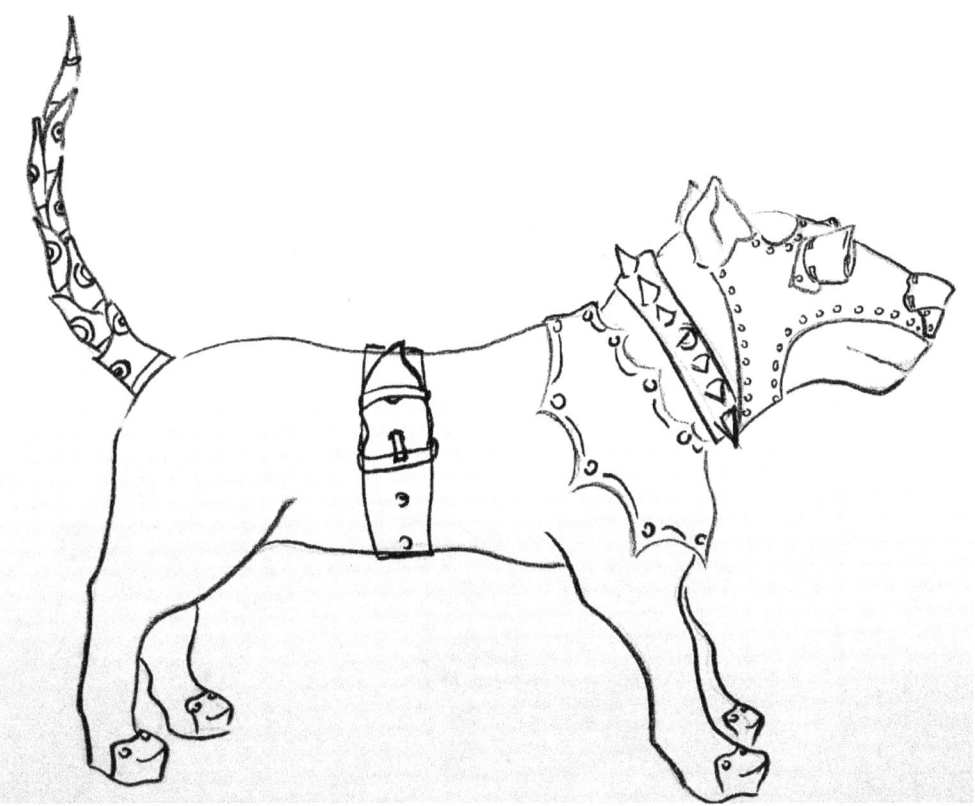

Step 5

Give shading in the metal plate drawn on the shoulder and the belt drawn on the chest.

Draw one casing each on the feet of Granger and depict two fasteners on each casing. The casing should be drawn such that they are meant to protect the feet of this warrior dog.

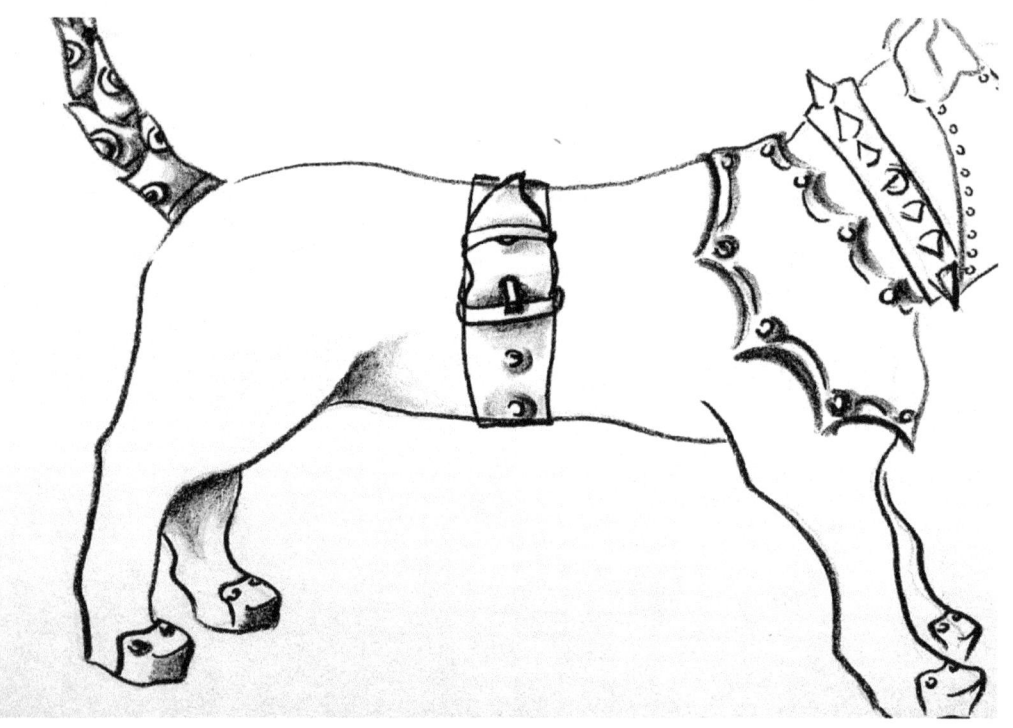

Step 6

Give shading in the body of Granger as shown in the picture. Keep the shading to the minimum so that the accessories are highlighted more. The shading in the tail should be done precisely as this is the most important part of this animal.

The sketch of this Steampunk dog, Granger, is complete.

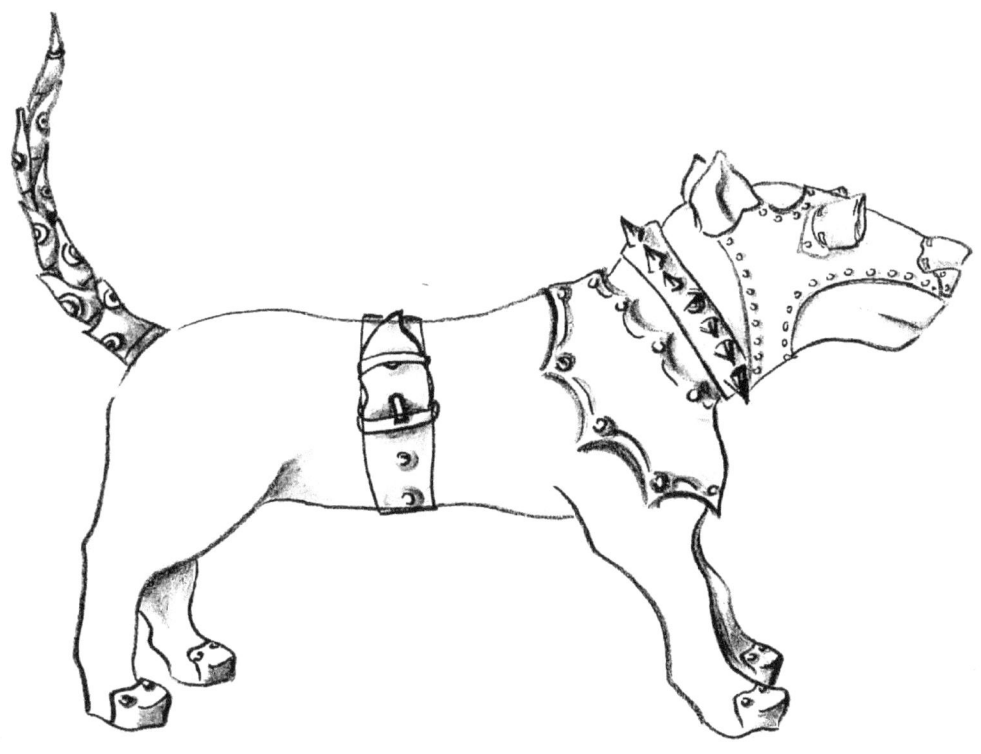

Chapter 6 - Watson

Watson dresses up like he is very dangerous, but he is a very playful dog.

And, he knows how to behave in front of his master's friends.

Step 1

Draw the outline of this steampunk dog, Watson. The tail has some graduating chips insterted on it. The left ear has a few staples on its edges. You can see that there are different patches drawn on the face. We will draw different embellishments on these patches later. Draw one fastener below the left ear and another fastener beneath the previous one.

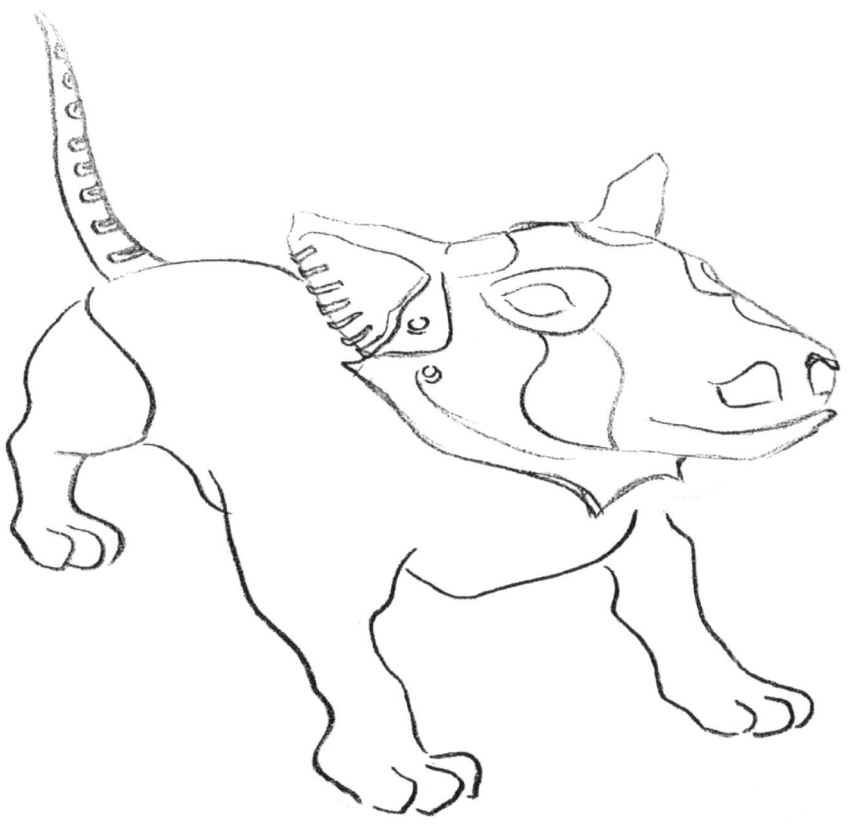

Step 2

Draw a string of beads around the eyes and darken the inner portion of the eye, sclera, which is normally white in humans. The right eye is not visible to us completely. Thus, you must draw the sclera and the string of beads around it in perspective.

Draw a coiled wire emerging from the plate located on the throat of Watson and connecting in his mouth.

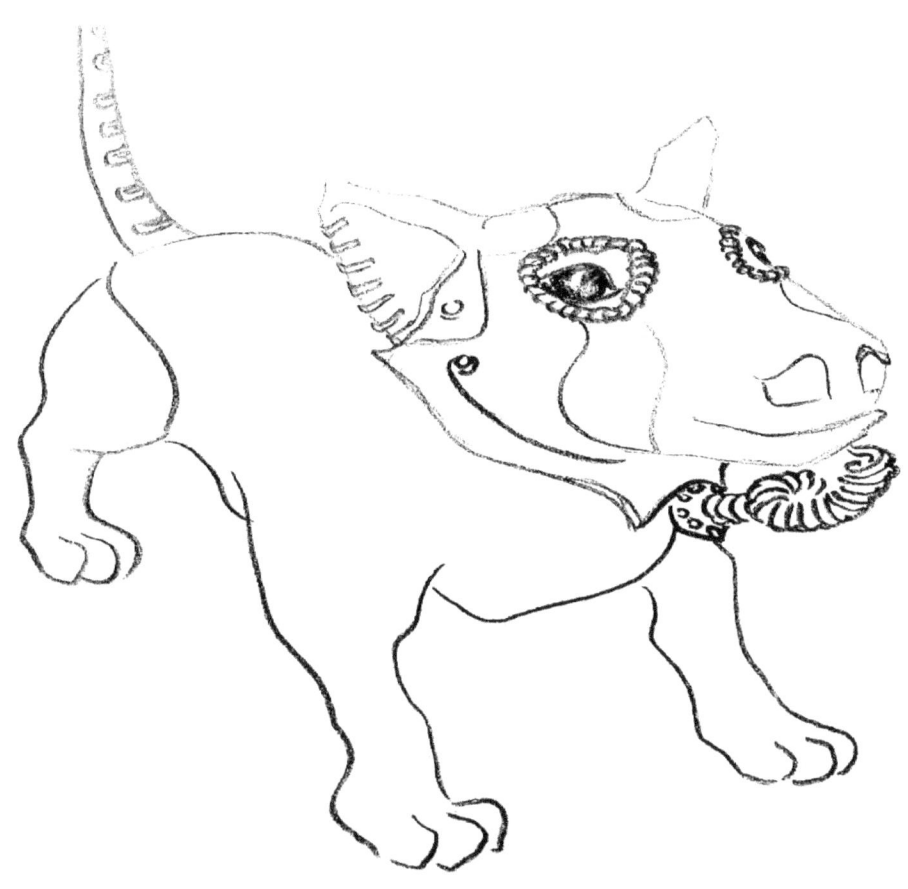

Step 3

Draw two sets of "S" shaped lines parallel to each other emerging from the left eye and reaching the chin. Draw a line between the eyes dividing the face into two parts. Draw some vertical chips parallel to this line.

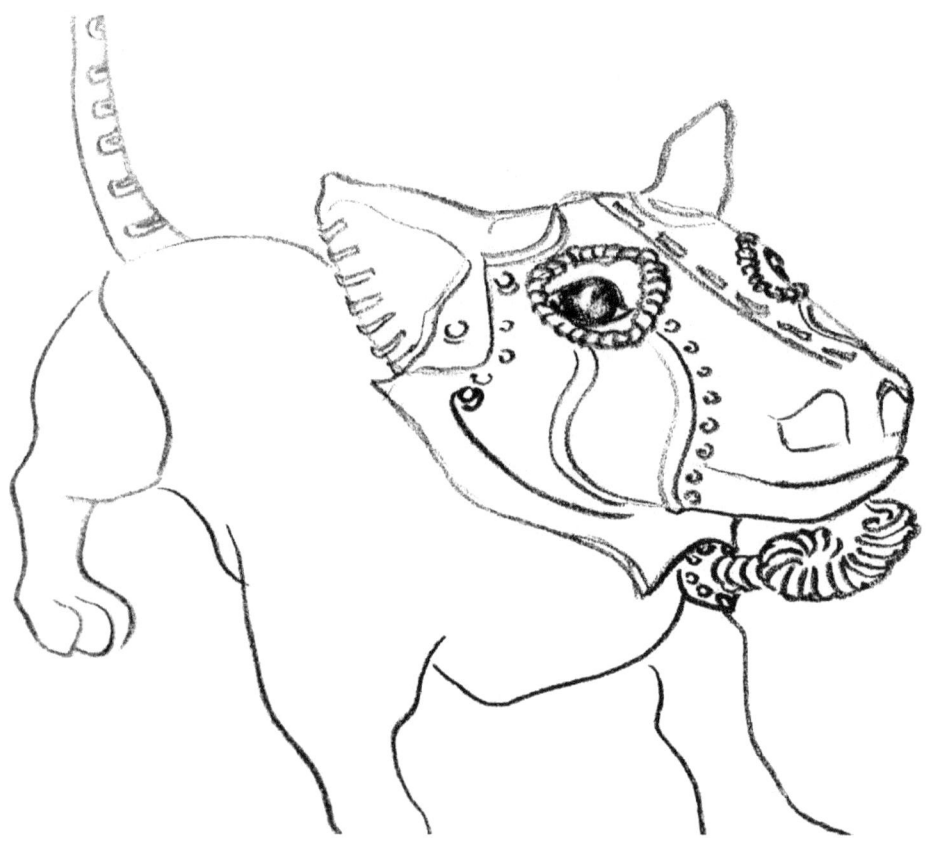

Step 4

On the left hind leg, draw some screw like shapes placed adjacent to each other. Draw a half gear beneath these screws. Draw three chips on the joint of this same leg. On the "S" shaped lines on the face, draw fasteners along one line. Draw running stitches along the other "S" line.

Draw a collar around the neck of Watson and place some running stitches along its edges.

On the front legs draw lines parallel to each other as if there is a "corset" being worn on the legs.

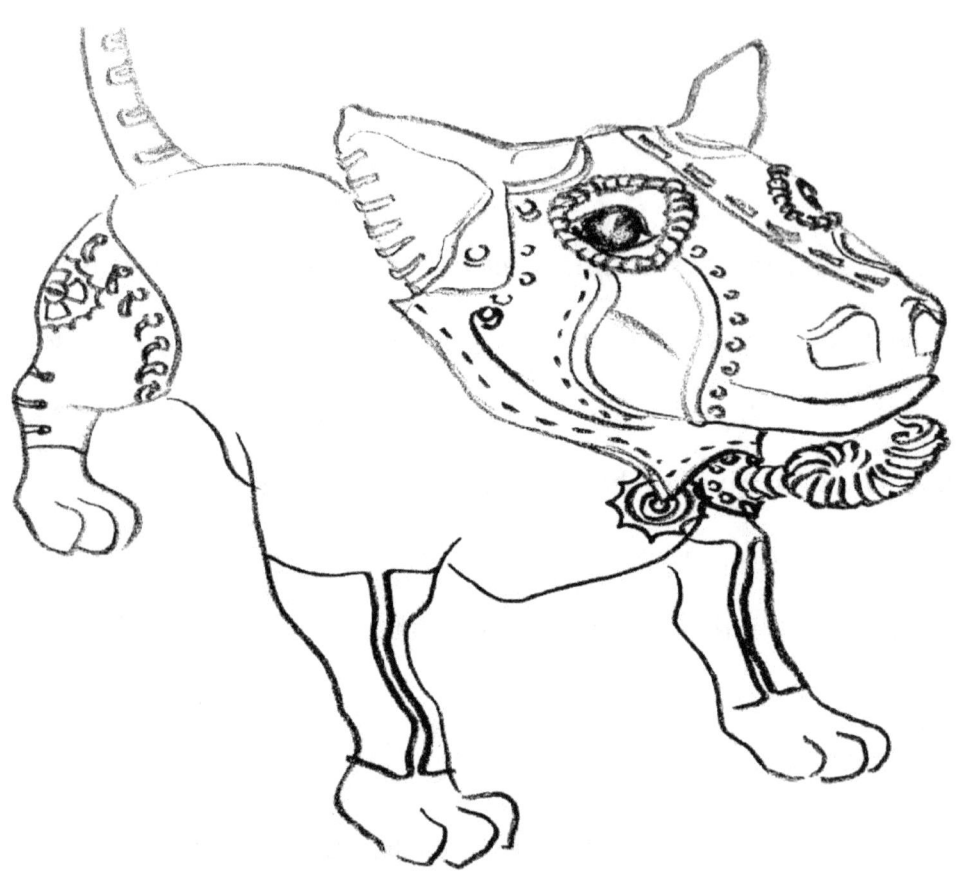

Step 5

Draw some piercing holes on the "corset" of the front legs and draw thread passing through these holes. The whole thing should look like the corset is being held by these stitches.

Give light shading in the face, legs and tail.

The sketch of the Steampunk dog, Watson, is complete.

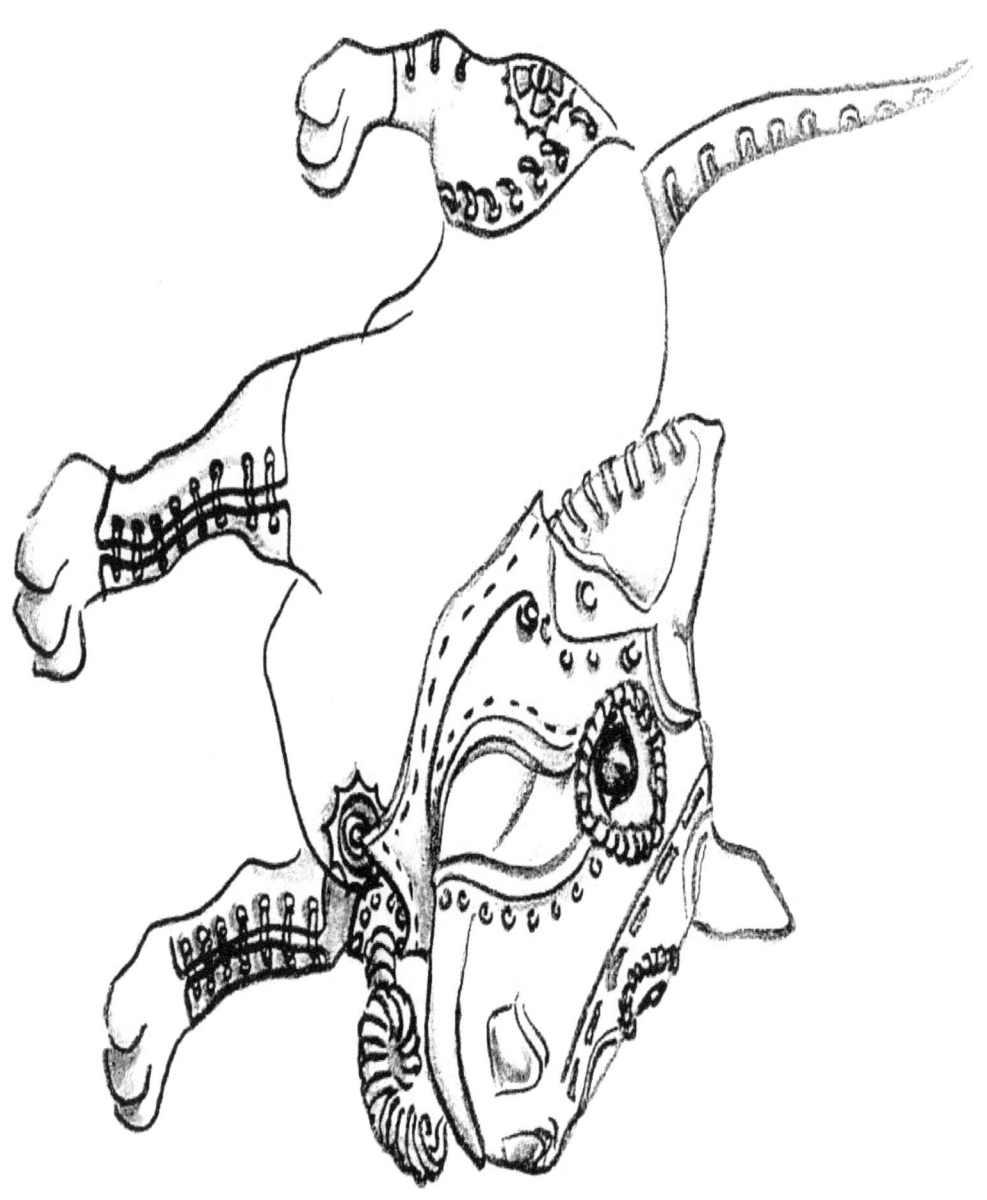

Conclusion

Everything about dogs is just so entertaining, whether it is playing with them, photographing them, sketching them, reading or writing about them. They are such adorable creatures gifted to the human beings that we just cannot resists having them in our lives. Those who love dogs may even find the stray dogs adorable. There are many instances of such people who adopt pups from the streets and nurture them like their own kids.

Though for drawing Steampunk dogs, you do not necessarily have to own a pet; but it is better to take inspiration from dogs around you. You can even take reference from the plethora of pictures available online. But, it is better to take a print out of such pictures from Internet because when you sit down to draw, you will feel better to have a hard copy in front of you. The soft copy on your laptop or your Smartphone might not give you a good feeling of drawing. Another advantage of having a hard copy in front of you is that you can draw and mark some points on it if you want to. You can even make grids on it to help you in drawing if you are new at sketching dogs.

Making grids is a very convenient and effective method of drawing any kind of sketches. It also helps you to attain perfection sooner than any other method. Learn this method by heart if you do not know much about it.

Go through other art forms as well which depict dogs as their main subject. This will help you to draw them in different positions. In the first section of **Steampunk Dogs: Drawing Steampunk Dogs,** you must have read about Michael Sowa, who depicts dogs and other animals as the main subject of his paintings. You can research more about this artist and take inspiration from his paintings. Also, if you search about Steampunk dogs, you will find many real life dogs, which are accessorized as Steampunk figures. Learn from these pictures how to accessorize your sketches of Steampunk dogs.

There is no harm in learning from whichever source you can. Now that you have read all the tutorials of Steampunk dogs, you must have noticed that each dog can be assigned a special character just with the help of the accessories, despite their natural features. You can experiment with different accessories and give a unique character to all your sketches. Just keep an observant eye on all the machinery around you and how their inner parts are assembled. In a few days only, you will start visualizing them in your mind as to how you can incorporate them in your sketches. Keep practicing to attain perfection in Steampunk drawings.

Enjoy this journey as much as you can and it will no longer seem like work!

Other books by Jeffrey Stains

STEAMPUNK:

Drawing Amazing Steampunk Figures!
Book 1

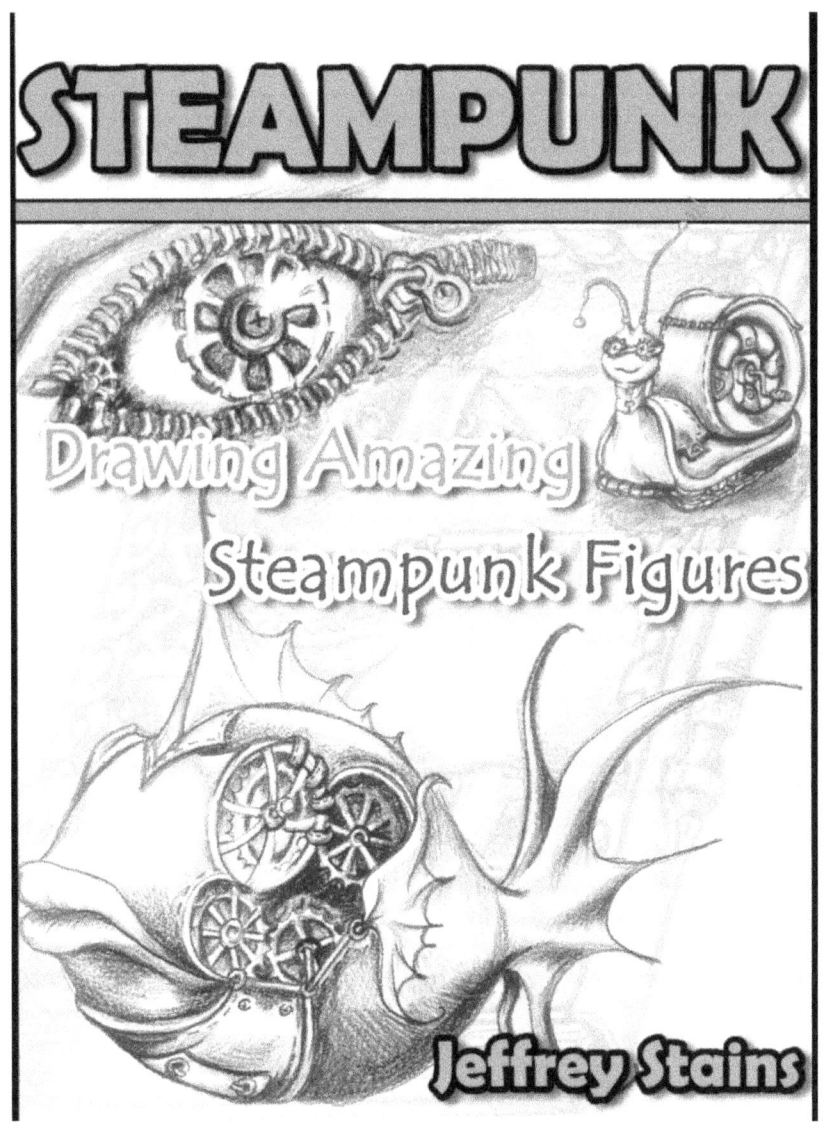

Steampunk:

Learn How to Draw
Amazing Steampunk Figures!
Book 2

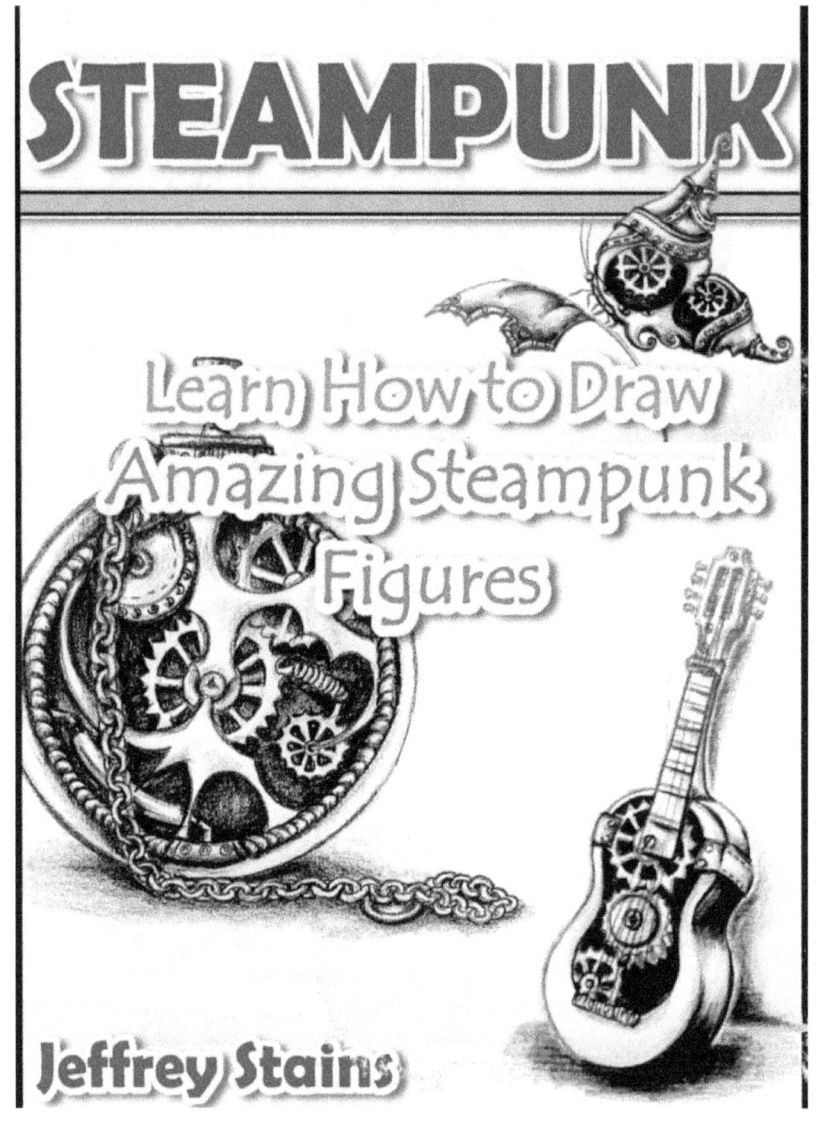

STEAMPUNK CATS Drawing:

A Completely New Form of Cats!

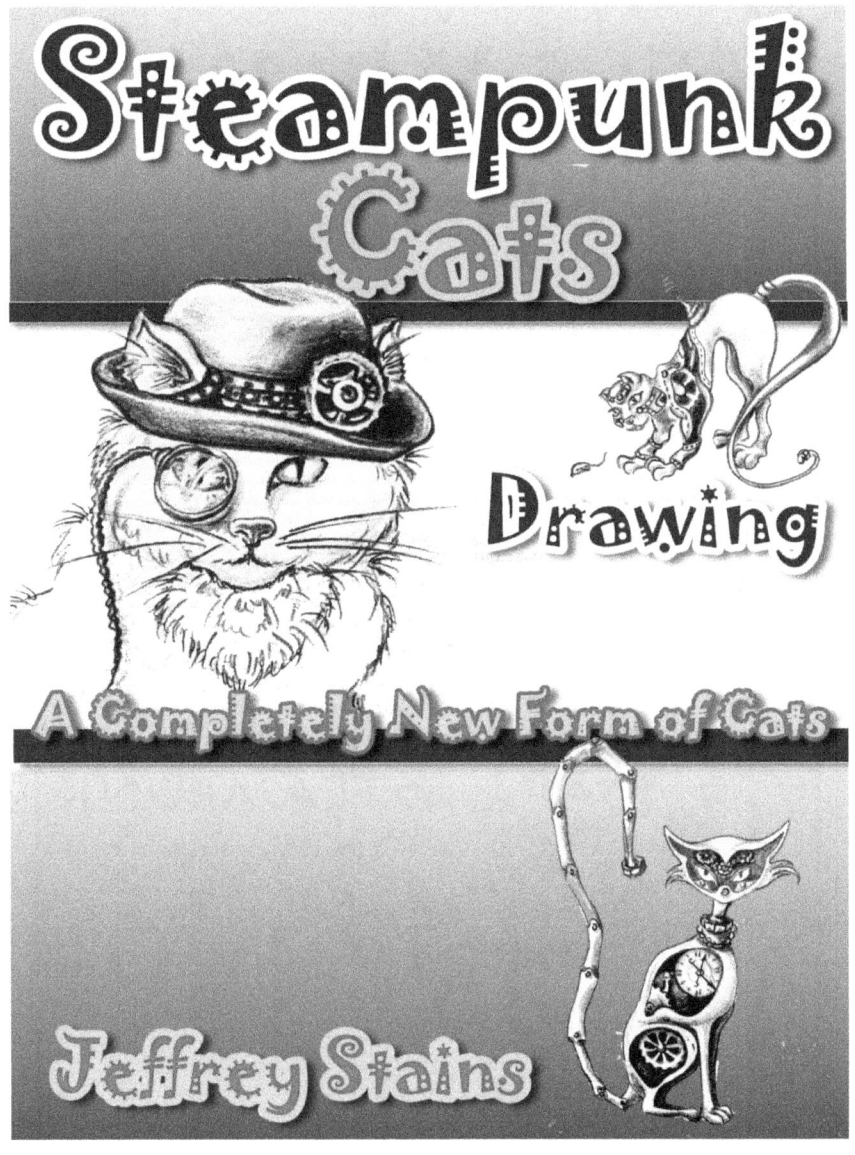

Steampunk Animals:

Sketching Steampunk Animals with Creative Steampunk Drawings!

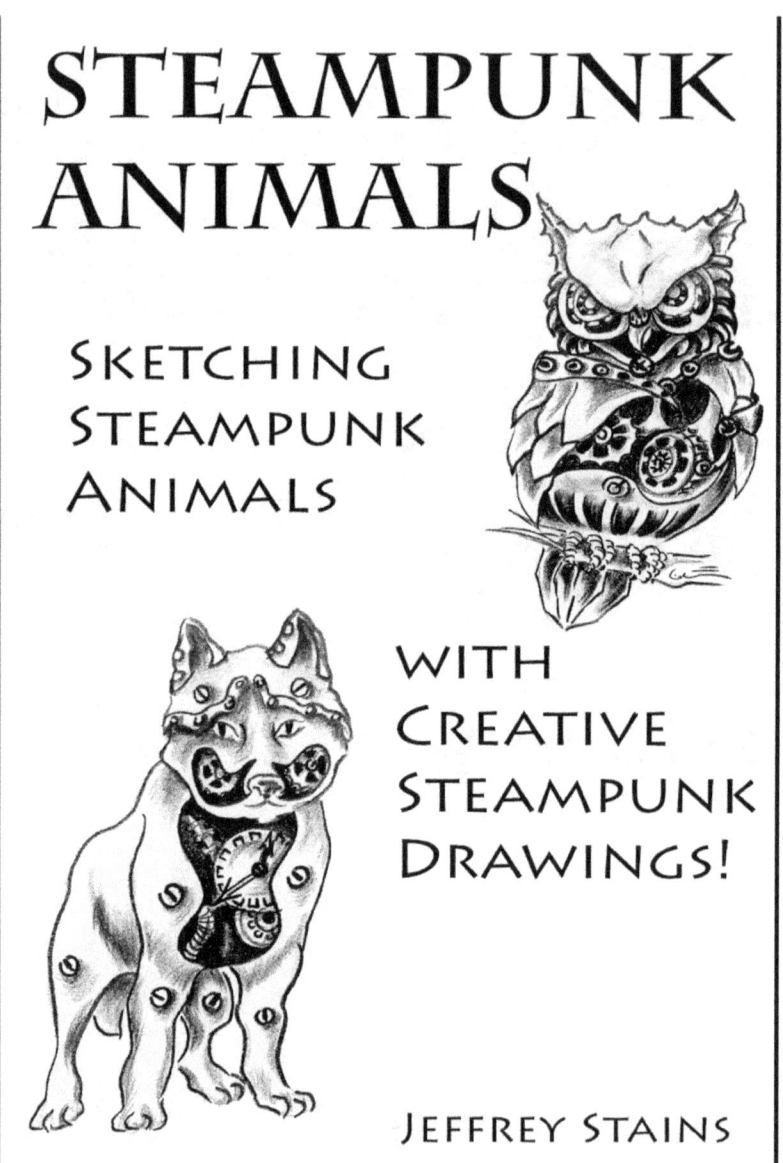

Thank you!

Thank you for choosing our book, we hope you found it interesting and helpful.
If you liked the book, please give us a favor to write your review.

We would really appreciate this!

If you would like to have a bonus – **FREE BOOK**, please send the screenshot of your review to this e-mail:

kelly.artbooks@gmail.com and we
will send you a **FREE BOOK** in PDF as a **GIFT!****

Hope to see you in our future books and good luck in your drawing experience!

** **in the e-mail subject please mention the name of the book you reviewed and the author.**

www.ingramcontent.com/pod-product-compliance
Lightning Source LLC
Chambersburg PA
CBHW080724190526

45169CB00006B/2508